Nonnie
Talks about
Disability

Suggested for children in grades 3-8 and their trusted adults

An Interactive Book for Children and Adults

By Dr. Mary Jo Podgurski

Consultant Kendle Haught

Illustrations by Alice M. Burroughs

One Kid at A Time

NONNIE TALKS ABOUT DISABILITY: VOLUME NINE OF THE NONNIE SERIES

ISBN: 978-1-7343001-0-9

Dedication

This one is dedicated with all my love to three of my grandbabies:
Jai, Lily and Evan

Thank you to my generous, wise reviewers:
Nancy Aloi
Cindy Lee Alves
Jeffrey Anthony
Lexx Brown James
LaShauna Carruthers
Darrilyn McCreary
Shawn Sellers
Aaminah Shakur
Sarah Slough
Bill Taverner

Thank you to my self-advocate consultants:
Jimmy Belcastro
Kristen Bennett
Princess Johnson
Cheryl Parrino

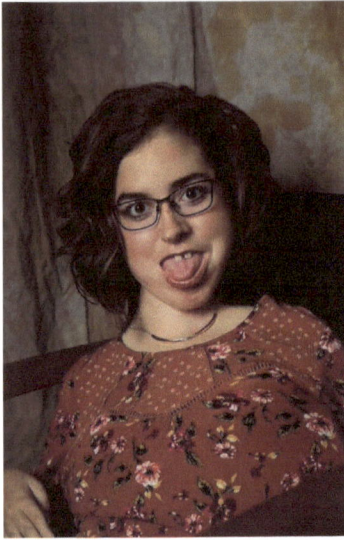

About Consultant Author Kendle Haught

Kendle Haught is seventeen years old. She enjoys listening to music, using social media, and just being a teenager.

At five months old, she was diagnosed with Merosin Negative Congenital Muscular Dystrophy. She has driven a power wheelchair since the age of 2 1/2. There have been many obstacles in her life between surgeries, broken bones, and reoccurring respiratory illnesses, yet she remains positive and always has a smile on her face.

She is a high school senior this year, and can not wait to see what her future holds!! Kendle applied to three colleges and has already been accepted by all three! (10/2019)

Kendle's Words

I was so honored when I was asked to be a part of this book and I could not agree more with its message.

I enjoyed so much working with Dr. Mary Jo Podgurski throughout this time of creating the book.

I was most excited to be able to put my character out there and have it be as raw and as real as possible.

I am looking forward to being a part of such a legacy this Nonnie series brings with its name!!

I love writing all the books in The Nonnie Series™, but this one truly touched my heart.

The 9th Volume in The Nonnie Series™ looks at the world of disability.

Some children and young people live in a complicated or protected world, where they may not encounter disabled individuals. Some children don't know how to act when they meet someone with a disability. Other children live with disabilities. This book seeks to create a learning tool for adults and young people where open conversation about disabilities and disabled young people can freely occur.

In selecting 17-year-old Kendle Haught as my consulting author, I partnered with someone who lives an authentic life as a disabled teen. Kendle's insight was key to this book's birth. As always in my Nonnie Series, I wrote the dialogue and then gave it to Kendle for feedback. She was exceptional. She'd say things like "This is great! I would say that," and then gently add, "How about saying this?"

Kendle was a peer educator with my program before I asked her to work on *Nonnie Talks about Disability.* Not only did she want to be a character in the book, she wanted the character to be as real as possible. This is a unique book because of her involvement.

The other new characters in the book – LaShauna, David, Dylan and Malik – are also real young people, although David, Dylan and Malik's names are changed. LaShauna is a dynamite peer educator, which is perfect in the progression of the Series. Both Tamika and Alex are named for peer educators I worked with over 20 years ago.

May I ask readers to explore human difference with young people in this book?
Use the book to learn about the lives and accessibility needs of young people with physical disabilities, autistic teens, teens living with Down syndrome and Deaf young people.

Then, please model respect for all people. Each Person is A Person of Worth.

I wish you joy.
Mary Jo

Many people ask me for help in determining a child's readiness for the books in the Nonnie Series.

Children today can glean information from online sources in a mouse click or smartphone search, but they are not always as comfortable sharing their concerns with adults. Adults, conversely, may not know how to address complicated topics, or may think a child is "too young" or unaware. I think the power of the Nonnie Series is the message "It's OK to talk about this together" – for adults and children!

Monitor your children's ability to process information. Maturity and age are often unrelated to reading ability; an adult can read and explain complicated words and concepts, but a child's curiosity and eagerness to embrace knowledge are important considerations. Adults need to "articulate the obvious" when educating children. It's important to empower. Too often adults think the word empower means they give power to young people; the opposite is true. When we empower young people, we guide them to find their own power.

Try paraphrasing this message: "I'd like to look at this book with you. I think you may be interested in the topic. We can read the book at your own pace. You can talk with me about anything, and I will respect you. I will always respect your feelings."

I suggest grade levels as opposed to age because I'm sensitive to reading ability, but I truly do not feel the books should be limited to one group. For example, not all third- or fourth-graders will be developmentally ready for all the chapters in the books; the books should be read at a child's speed. On the other hand, not all seventh- or eighth-graders will be interested in interacting with an adult to address these topics, but some will enjoy learning and communicating with someone they trust. I hold focus groups with children from grades 3-8 prior to writing a Nonnie book to ascertain the book's developmental content.

No one is more important to a child than a trusted adult. Learning takes place when we process information; communicate with the young people in your life and share your values with respect.

Each child is different. Let your children lead you. Their interest, more than their grade level or age, should be your guide.

Thank you for listening and caring about young people.

With respect and admiration,

Mary Jo Podgurski

Dr. Mary Jo Podgurski

Nonnie
Talks about
Disability

Suggested for children in grades
3-8 and their trusted adults

By Dr. Mary Jo Podgurski

Consultant Kendle Haught

Illustrations by Alice M. Burroughs

One
Kid at A
Time™

HOW TO USE THIS BOOK:

Nonnie Talks about Disability was created to be used by children and adults together. Please read this book with someone who matters to you.

For Children:

This picture means you may color the page if you wish. This symbol * or a red word means a word may be new. The Glossary on pages 70-75 will help with new words. Words written in blue are especially important messages or are for you, the reader. Groups of words marked with a small number above the words (like this³) refer to a footnote (a sentence at the bottom of the page) to explain something in more detail.

A What do YOU think? page is a great page to help people talk with each other.
Please talk with a trusted adult!
Please listen!

Most important:
Every person is different.
Each child who picks up this book is different.
Each adult who reads this book with a child is different.
Some ideas may be easy to understand. That's OK.
Some ideas may be difficult to understand. That's OK.

 AcademyPress ~ http://www.healthyteens.com/

HOW TO USE THIS BOOK:

FOR PARENTS, TEACHERS AND TRUSTED ADULTS:

1. I strongly recommend reading the book without your child first. Consider any concerns you may have with the material and prepare for your child's possible questions.

2. The book is divided into chapters. The chapters are only suggestions; they divide the content to allow for pleasant learning. The book may be read as one part, two parts, three parts, four parts—it's up to you. You know your children best. Please monitor their attention, their interest, and their awareness and understanding of the concepts.

3. The topic of disability is a critical issue in today's world. Teaching acceptance for difference and empathy for another's life experiences are key components to developing a positive person. You are your child's first teacher. Communicate!

4. As Tamika and Alex discuss, disability is complicated and intense. Disabled people are not less than others, but have their own unique gifts and points of view. No one should be invisible.

5. The Appendixes (pages 66-69) include food for thought for your reading pleasure. You may want to share these concepts with children who are cognitively ready for them.

6. Just as children's physical and emotional development are unique, so is their readiness for information. Please let the children you love be your guides.

7. The What do YOU Think? pages should be completed at a child's pace, but are important. Learning takes place when we process information.

Most important:

Be aware of the "music" (tone of voice) behind your words. Adult modeling and acceptance of skills like respect and empathy as an ally are vital.

Please teach children the importance of respect.

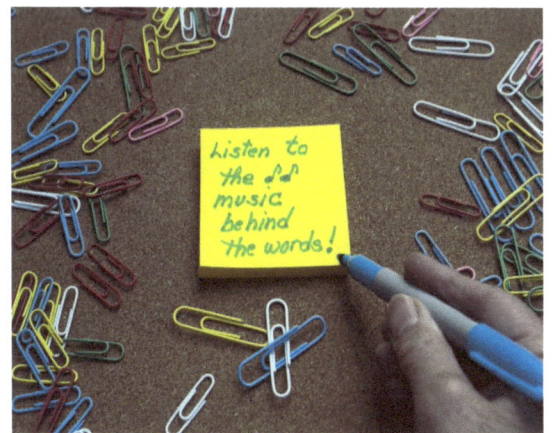

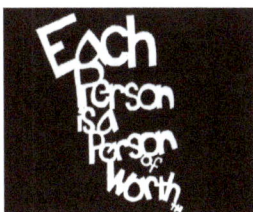

Listen to the ♪♫ music behind the words!

Each Person is a Person of Worth. Please pass it on!

Mary Jo Podgurski

AcademyPress ~ http://www.healthyteens.com/

Chapter One: The Story Begins

Did you ever have a
huge question?

Most children wonder about a
lot of different things.

Would you like to read a story
about two children with lots of questions?
The story may answer some of your
questions.

If you still have questions when the story is finished,
please ask your parents or a trusted adult.

1

AcademyPress ~ http://www.healthyteens.com/

Once upon a time....

Alex and Tamika are best friends.

They can't remember a time when they weren't friends.

Their parents said they were even in the same play group when they were only two years old! As they grow older, their friendship also changes and grows.

 AcademyPress ~ http://www.healthyteens.com/

Alex and Tamika are very curious. When something confuses them or makes them wonder, they often turn to the trusted adults in their families for answers.

They speak with their parents, Tamika's older brother, their aunts and uncles, and their teachers and other trusted adults.

A trusted adult is someone who respects young people, listens to their thoughts, and keeps promises.

Alex's grandma is a nurse and a teacher and a counselor.

Tamika and he call her Nonnie. When they're confused or curious about something they often talk with Nonnie. She listens to them, respects them, and helps them grow and learn. She is a trusted adult.

WHAT DO YOU THINK? Have you ever wanted to talk with a trusted adult? Who are the trusted adults in your life?

AcademyPress ~ http://www.healthyteens.com/

Alex and Tamika are starting 7th grade.

Friendships are very important to them now.

They care about what their friends think about them.

They spend a lot of time thinking about how they dress for school and activities. They text and talk on the phone a lot!

Because Tamika and Alex taught their peers a little last year, they decided to begin formal training as peer educators.

Peer educators teach and model healthy choices to other young people. Nonnie says, "When an adult teaches young people, the message is heard as a whisper. When a peer educator teaches, it's heard as a shout."

They can't wait to attend the peer educator training.

   AcademyPress ~ http://www.healthyteens.com/

What do YOU Think?

How important are friendships to you?

Do you think you'd like to teach your peers?
Why or why not?
Do you like talking in front of others?
How can you help your peers learn what they need?

Please draw
or write your
thoughts
here:

AcademyPress ~ http://www.healthyteens.com/

Chapter Two: Learning to Teach

Nonnie's peer educator trainings are 12 total hours, divided into two hour sessions. Each week the new peer educators grow as facilitators and discussion leaders.

Tamika and Alex were excited to spend time with their friends at the Teen Center training.

Two new friends joined them. LaShauna and Kendle attend different schools but are united in their desire to teach others.

First, the group played a game to get to know each other.
They threw squishy balls back and forth as they introduced themselves.

They also shared their favorite song.
Tamika sang her favorite tune.
She likes to sing.

   AcademyPress ~ http://www.healthyteens.com/

Tamika read the group's mission.

She said, "The mission of the Peer Educators is to inspire, educate, respect and advocate for young people by empowering teens to make healthy choices, become contributing members of their communities, and make social change." She looked at her friends and asked, "What do you think that means?"

LaShauna said, "It means we are role models for other teens. They watch what we do and copy us."

Alex said, "I think it also means we need to learn new things so we can pass them on to our peers."

Kendle asked, "Nonnie, what do we do first?"

Nonnie smiled. "Great teaching is interactive, so the first thing we need to do is create a safe space where everyone is respected and engaged."

SAFE Everyone
©2016 MJ Podgurski, RNC, EdD

Nonnie asked, "What would help you feel safe in a class?"

AcademyPress ~ http://www.healthyteens.com/

Alex said, "Knowing I can be myself and be respected."

Tamika said, "Being able to speak about anything I wanted."

Nonnie nodded, "What else?"

Kendle said, "Knowing I won't be judged for what I say or how I look."

"Excellent," said Nonnie.

LaShauna was quiet. The others knew she was thinking. She looked at Tamika and said, "Maybe a safe space is a place where people can have courageous conversations."

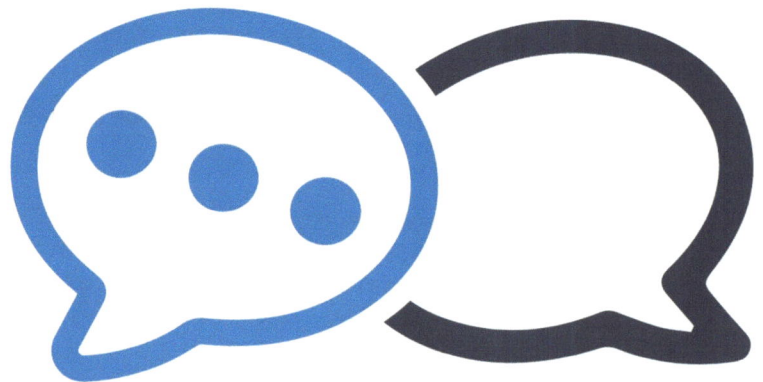

Tamika agreed. "We learned about courageous conversations in social studies class, Nonnie."

"I'm glad," Nonnie looked very happy. "What makes a conversation courageous?"

"Mr. B said a person speaks their truth during a courageous conversation," said Kendle.

LaShauna said, "It might take courage just to bring up a topic."

8

 AcademyPress ~ http://www.healthyteens.com/

Tamika added, "You can bring up topics or problems that are difficult to talk about during a courageous conversation."

Alex said, "You need to be brave enough to think about things that make you uncomfortable."

LaShauna agreed. "Some topics are tough. Having a courageous conversation can clear the air."

Nonnie asked, "What makes a topic tough to discuss?"

Tamika laughed, "Some people say to avoid talking about politics and religion."

"What do you think?" Nonnie was curious.

Tamika shrugged. "I think if we don't find the courage to talk about things we won't learn to respect each other."

Alex said, "Sometimes we need to learn to agree to disagree with respect."

Kendle spoke up, "I think we need to talk about our differences." She looked determined. "It's important to stand for what we believe."

Alex agreed, but then said, "I guess sometimes you just disagree."

9

What do YOU Think?

Do you agree? Should we talk about our differences? Why would it take courage to do so? Why do you think some people are afraid to talk about differences?

Does talking about any topic make you feel uneasy? Which topics are the most complicated?

Please draw or write your thoughts here:

10

AcademyPress ~ http://www.healthyteens.com/

Chapter Three: Perspective

Nonnie smiled but her words were serious. "I think the more we communicate the more we can connect." She watched the new peer educators closely. "We also need to be aware of another's perspective." She asked them, "What do you think?"

LaShauna quickly said, "I think Kendle is right. We should talk about our differences so we learn to respect each other."

Kendle said, "I like what you said about perspective Nonnie. I like the idea of trying to see things from other people's point of view. I do think talking about religion can be courageous. People sometimes hate others who believe differently."

*See Appendix #1

LaShauna said, "I'm a Christian, but I respect all people's beliefs."

Tamika agreed. "I made a new friend at the last Math Counts. She's Jewish. I told her we went to visit a synagogue when Nonnie taught us about death.[1] She's taking me to her synagogue for a Sabbath service."

"I remember," said Alex. "We also visited a mosque and a Buddhist temple." He paused thinking. "There are many world religions, and some people may not follow a religion."

Kendle asked, "What other differences should we consider?"

[1] See *Nonnie Talks about Death* for more information

*

 AcademyPress ~ http://www.healthyteens.com/

Nonnie noticed Kendle facilitating the group and was pleased. She also wondered if Kendle was trying to get the others to think about something.

Tamika said, "Race and ethnicity. People judge others by the color of their skin. We've learned racism is real."[2]

"Or people are judged by the language they speak," added Alex.

Nonnie sighed. "When my Papa came to America from Italy he was only 14. He immigrated from a town near Naples. He was mocked for speaking English poorly."

Nonnie smiled. "He was so determined to speak English he wouldn't teach me Italian. He did cuss in Italian so I wouldn't learn swear words in English. So, I learned them in Italian!"

Everyone laughed, picturing Nonnie's father with a swear jar for Italian words.

Barattolo di Parolacce*

Tamika said, "I know people who judge because someone wears less expensive clothes …"

*Jar of bad words in Italian
[2] See *Nonnie Talks about Race* for more information

AcademyPress ~ http://www.healthyteens.com/

"Or judge by the type of car someone drives…." said LaShauna

"Or by how much money they can spend…." added Alex.

Nonnie said, "People may also be judged by their ages. You're young people. Your voices may not be heard. We're preparing to teach your peers. Their voices may not be heard. I'm getting old. I may not be respected due to my age. We are all different ages, but not all of us receive the same respect."

They were all quiet. They couldn't imagine anyone disrespecting Nonnie.

Kendle asked, "Are there any other areas where people are judged because they're different?"

The others thought about her question. "Maybe we judge others based on how smart they are?" Alex asked.

"Or tests scores," Nonnie agreed. "Not everyone likes taking tests."

All the peer educators groaned. "Even if I do well," Tamika said, "Taking tests can be stressful!"

AcademyPress ~ http://www.healthyteens.com/

"What about athletic ability?" asked Tamika. "We always seem to judge people by how well they play sports. Or if they're involved in sports at all."

LaShauna said, "Agreed, and we often are judged because of our gender."[4]

"Yes," said Nonnie. "Anything else?" she asked.

Alex said, "I know people who hate a person just because of their sexual orientation."

Tamika agreed. "Like who we're attracted to or who we fall in love with or we like." She smiled at Nonnie. "You taught us about sexual stuff before."[5]

Nonnie asked, "What do you know about privilege?"

LaShauna answered. "When one person has advantages or is treated better than others because of something like the color of their skin or their sexuality or gender."

Alex added, "We learned about white privilege, Nonnie, when you taught us about race. And I know about heterosexual and cisgender privilege. Are there other kinds of privilege?"

[4] See *Nonnie Talks about Gender* for more information
[5] See *Nonnie Talks about Sex...& More* for more information

 AcademyPress ~ http://www.healthyteens.com/

Chapter Four: Privilege and Stereotypes

Nonnie said, "Everyone has some type of privilege."

Now Kendle stopped to think. She was quiet. She's a talker, so Tamika paid extra attention to her to make sure she was OK.

"My friend Josh says he doesn't have any privilege," said Alex. "I tried to argue with him but he got mad and then I got mad and so we stopped talking about it"

LaShauna said, "Remember when you talked about respecting others, Alex?"

Alex snorted. "Yeah," he said. "It's way easier to talk about doing something than to actually do it."

EASIER SAID
Than Done

Nonnie said gently. "Very true, Alex. Many people miss the point of privilege. They think it means there's only one type. It seems most people think about race or gender or money.

In truth, there are many ways one group of people has more power than another. You mentioned some. Privilege is connected to stereotypes and isms."

Tamika was excited, "Remember when we did the lesson on Smash the Stereotypes? We discussed isms. You're right, Nonnie," she said, "We're talking about a lot of isms right now!"

 AcademyPress ~ http://www.healthyteens.com/

"Things like ageism and sexism and anti-Semitism," Alex said.

They thought of the art contest they held last year as part of peer ed. The winner was a high school student named Kacy Barton. Her artwork looked like this:

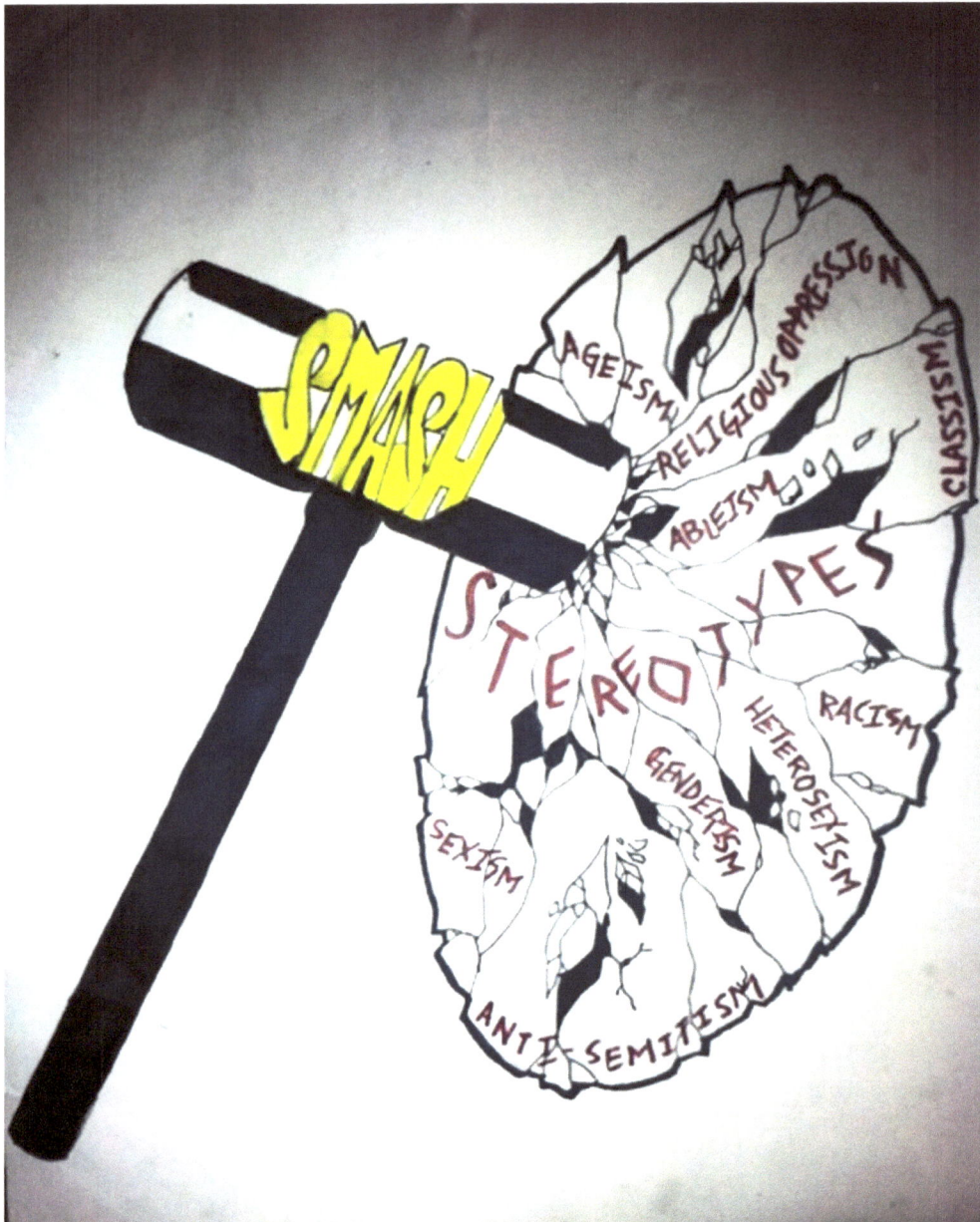

Kendle spoke up. "There are a lot if isms," she said. "I think you're missing a big one."

Kendle moved her hand and made an imaginary circle around her wheelchair. The others stared.

 AcademyPress ~ http://www.healthyteens.com/

Kendle was careful. She sensed her friends were uncomfortable. "I'm often judged by my disability," she said. "People sometimes even talk loudly to me, as if my physical abilities make me unable to hear! Sometimes I feel like shouting, 'I CAN HEAR!'"

Tamika was quick to speak, feeling awful. "Do they really shout? That's horrible!"

"Like they're using a megaphone," Kendle gave them a little smile. "Didn't any of you ever notice."

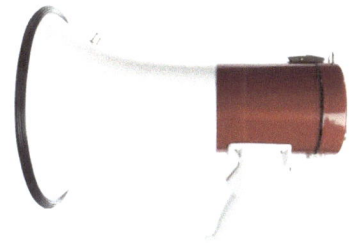

Everyone felt awkward.

"I know you didn't mean to forget me." Kendle continued, "Sometimes," she hesitated. Nonnie gently said, "You can feel safe saying anything with us, Kendle."

Kendle nodded. "I don't ever want to be invisible."

Shocked, LaShauna shook her head, "We see you," she said. "You're our friend."

Alex added, "Maybe that's why we didn't even think to mention disability. We just see you as one of us."

Kendle said. "That's what ableism is. You all are able to do things I can't, but you didn't notice because of your own privilege."

 AcademyPress ~ http://www.healthyteens.com/

They all talked about how Kendle felt invisible. They decided to treat others with more respect.

The next day, Nonnie, Tamika and Alex took Alex's little sister Alisha to the mall to buy her new shoes.

They saw a woman using a wheelchair.

Alisha pointed at the woman and said, "Why does that lady sit in a chair? How can she make the chair move all by itself with no one pushing her?"

Alex and Tamika were embarrassed. They felt awkward and self-conscious.

Tamika whispered, "Alisha, it's not nice to point."

   AcademyPress ~ http://www.healthyteens.com/

Chapter Five: A Teachable Moment

Alisha stopped pointing, but said, "I just want to know."

They quickly met Nonnie in the food court where they'd planned to connect.

Nonnie took one look at their faces and knew something was wrong. Tamika looked miserable. Alex was quiet and he also looked upset. Alisha ran to Nonnie and said, "Tamika is mad at me."

"I'm not," protested Tamika.
Nonnie drew them to a table and ordered hot dogs.

She listened to each of them describe what happened, and then said, "This is a teachable moment for us all."

Alisha asked, "What's a teachable moment?"

Nonnie said, "A moment in life when we learn something."

Alisha's mouth opened in a wide O of surprise.

 AcademyPress ~ http://www.healthyteens.com/

Alisha said, "Nonnie, you don't need to learn anything. You know everything!"

Nonnie laughed so hard, Alex and Tamika and even Alisha started to laugh.

When they all settled down,
Alisha asked, "Are we laughing at me or at you, Nonnie?"

'Neither of us," Nonnie reassured. "We don't laugh *at* people, just *with* them. I laughed because I am constantly learning."

Alisha was puzzled. "But, you're old, Nonnie!" she said.

Tamika giggled, "That's ageism, right?"

Nonnie said, "In a way." She said it was OK to laugh together. She said curiosity was wonderful. She said children need answers to their questions even when the questions make adults feel uncomfortable.

She listened to Alisha's questions about the wheelchair.

She explained different abilities and said each person is worthy. She talked about respecting others.

WHAT DO YOU THINK? Did you ever notice, if someone is laughing a lot, you feel like laughing too? What if your friends are laughing AT someone? Do you laugh too?

20

        AcademyPress ~ http://www.healthyteens.com/

WHAT DO YOU THINK?

What do YOU Think?

Do you know any stereotypes? Why do you think the children forgot to talk about Kendle's physical disability?

Have you ever felt like Alex's sister Alisha felt when you saw someone different? Why was it easy to stare?

Please draw or write your thoughts here:

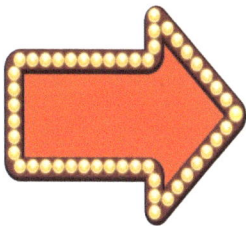

AcademyPress ~ http://www.healthyteens.com/

Nonnie said, "Let's go home and talk with Kendle for guidance. I wonder if we could've approached the woman Alisha saw respectfully and asked her to talk with Alisha. Let's see if Kendle agrees with that idea."

It was easy to meet with Kendle at the Teen Center, since the second peer educator training class was today.

Kendle had an easy answer to Alex's first question. He asked, "What should we do if Alisha points at someone again?"

Kendle said gently, "Alisha is learning. We need to teach her." She smiled. "I'm not sure talking with a stranger would make Alisha feel comfortable," she added. "I do know you can take her aside and teach her with care and respect. We all need to learn."

The others thanked Kendle. Alex asked, "What else can we do?"

Kendle smiled, "One thing that helps is making sure you don't talk at or down to a person using a wheelchair."

Tamika asked, "Help me with that, Kendle. What do you mean?

Kendle said, "Suppose we're talking. If we're going to speak for a while, please find a chair and sit at my level. It's weird to look up at someone when talking. It's easier to make eye contact if we're on the same level."

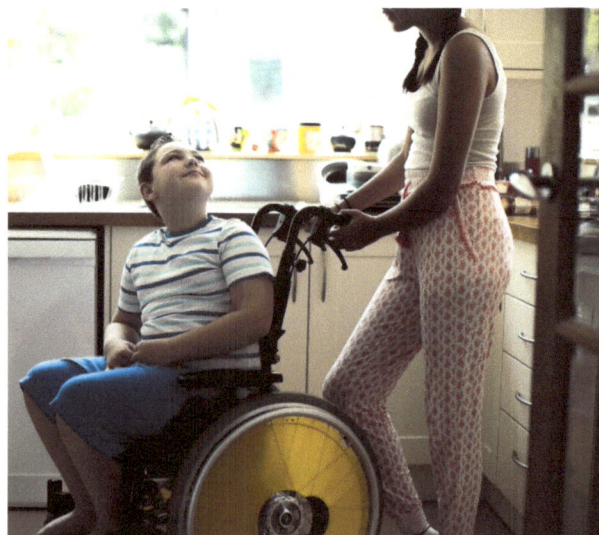

22

AcademyPress ~ http://www.healthyteens.com/

LaShauna said, "I've seen lots of people stand above those using wheelchairs at my work."

Kendle shook her head. "It's pretty common. People often assume things about disabled people. Like we don't understand or we're not able to do things."

Tamika nodded. "I get it. Like someone yelling at you."

"Or someone assuming you need help and trying to push your chair when it's electric and you can easily move from place to place." Alex grinned. "You can take care of yourself! I remember when you threatened to run over a kid's foot at the Teen Center because he was acting like a jerk!?"

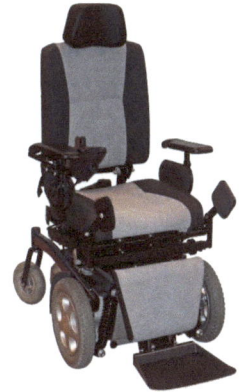

Kendle grinned too, and then was quiet. She suddenly looked sad.

"I'm glad you asked me my thoughts," she said. "Please remember I'm just one person who lives with a disability. I don't speak for everyone."

Nonnie quickly agreed. "How wise you are, Kendle! We shouldn't use our privilege to expect one person to speak for an entire group. This is true of race or gender or age or ability or any other group."

LaShauna said, "I remember you teaching us to read about other cultures and learn on our own.

23

Tamika said, "I get what you said, Kendle. Sometimes I'm the only Black kid in a class room and the teacher turns to me like I speak for all Black kids! I'm just me!"

LaShauna said, "Me too. It's like I'm supposed to speak for everyone."

Kendle said, "I do like to teach, though." She described a class her mom helped her create a few years ago. Every year, Kendle goes to the elementary school in her district and teaches first and second graders about disabilities.

She answers their questions about her chair and her life.

Tamika said, "Wow, Kendle. You're already a peer educator!"

Alex asked, "How did you know what to teach, Kendle?"

AcademyPress ~ http://www.healthyteens.com/

Kendle looked at Nonnie. She said, "It was like our conversation the other day. I thought about what I could say to help little children grow in kindness and respect. I showed them how my chair worked and let them ask me questions. I tried to put myself in their place. I tried to see why they were curious."

LaShauna was impressed. She said, "You were a great role model, Kendle. You showed the children you are worthy, just like them."

Nonnie said, "What do you think self-worth means?"

Alex said, "Feeling like you belong."

Tamika said, "Believing you can do something."

LaShauna said, "Knowing you're OK just as you are."

Kendle said, "Having the confidence to try something new."

Nonnie asked, "Is it easy to be confident?"

Tamika said softly, "Sometimes." She smiled. "Peer Ed helps!"

Kendle said, "Good friends help!"

AcademyPress ~ http://www.healthyteens.com/

Chapter Six: Accessibility

The rest of the peer educator class was spent preparing for their first teaching.

The new peer educators would go to Nonnie's college class to meet with students studying to be teachers. They would form a panel and talk about their experiences in 7th and 8th grade.

The school van dropped everyone off at the front of the building where Nonnie's education class met. Alex, Tamika and LaShauna easily ran to the doors. They held them open for Nonnie and Kendle.

There was only one problem.
The accessible ramp to enter the building wasn't OK.

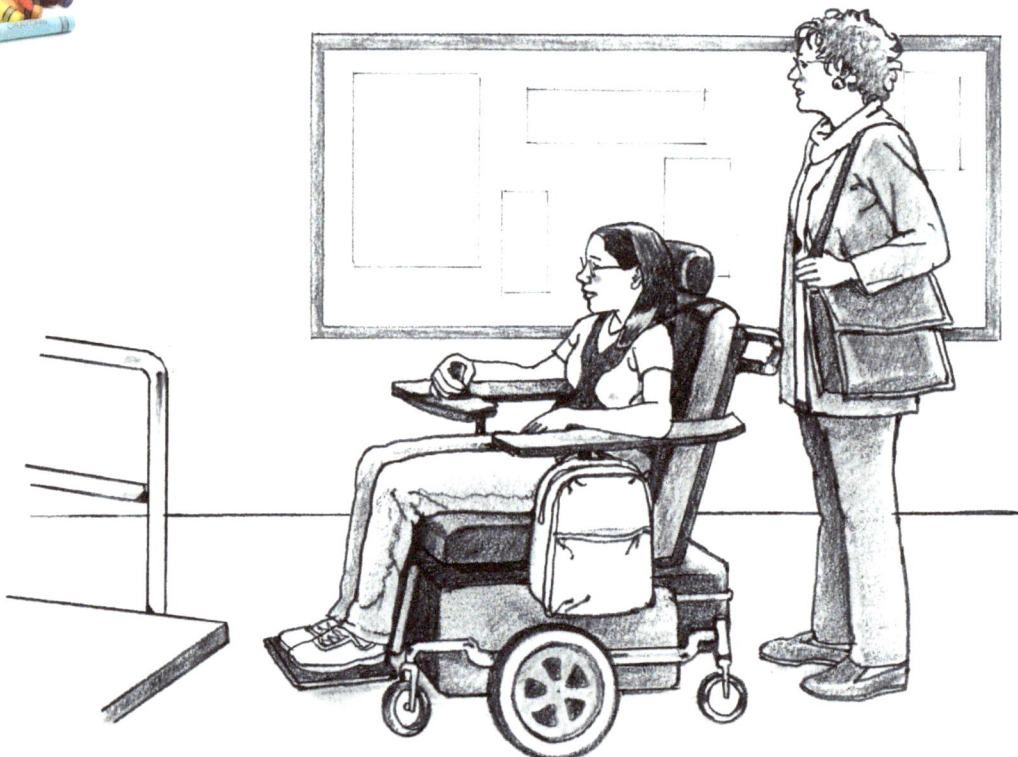

AcademyPress ~ http://www.healthyteens.com/

Kendle sighed, "This happens a lot," she said sadly.

Everyone returned to the van. They drove around to the back of the building. No luck. They drove back to the front of the building and tried to go over the ramp again—still too high.

Finally, a very nice maintenance person brought out a sturdy piece of wood and placed it over the ramp edge to make a more accessible entrance.

When they finally got into the building and to the elevator to go upstairs, Tamika mumbled, "That took forever."

Kendle nodded, "I'll bet you never noticed the ramp before," she said.

Alex agreed. "I never saw it through your eyes, Kendle."

Nonnie gave them a sad smile. She said. "There are so many ways accessibility is ignored. Can you think of some examples?"

LaShauna said, "What if the only way up in a building are stairs or an escalator?"

Kendle said, "Most larger buildings have an elevator. At times the only elevator is far away from where you need to go in a building, though."

 AcademyPress ~ http://www.healthyteens.com/

ACCESSIBLE ELEVATOR

Everyone thought about Kendle's words.

LaShauna said, "Isn't this about empathy?"

Alex agreed. "Nonnie, you taught us about empathy before. It's trying to 'get' what other people feel."

Tamika shook her head. "I just figured out something. I've used the accessible bathrooms in the past just because I liked the bigger stall," she said. "I won't do that again."

LaShauna added sadly, "It's as if we didn't notice things at all."

Nonnie said, "One way to look at privilege is to realize privilege means not having to think about something. Because you don't need an accessible entry way, you can walk past a ramp without thinking about whether it is actually accessible. We can use an accessible bathroom without thinking."

Privilege

 AcademyPress ~ http://www.healthyteens.com/

Kendle smiled. "Thanks," she said. "But, remember, disability isn't always easily seen. A person could be disabled and you wouldn't notice."

Nonnie smiled at Kendle. She asked, "Can you share what you mean by disability not always being seen?"

Kendle said, "Sure. Some disabilities aren't clear. For example, a person may live with a disability that makes them look like everyone else, but they're dealing with challenges."

Tamika asked, "Like someone with a learning disability? Our friend Sam at school needs extra time to learn things."

Nonnie said, "Right, Tamika. Can you think of another challenge we might not see?"

LaShauna said, "How about a mental health diagnosis? We can't see depression but it can be a true life challenge."

Alex said, "I'm starting to understand. We need to be more respectful to everyone." He added after a moment. "We should think more about *all* people's abilities— Disabled people are worthy. " The others agreed.

Their class went well. They felt closer and closer to being peer educators. Soon they would teach with Nonnie in a school.

 AcademyPress ~ http://www.healthyteens.com/

What do YOU Think?

Do you notice ramps and accessible bathrooms? Do you think your school would be an easy place for Kendle to attend? Why or why not?

If you were in charge of a school, how would you make it accessible for all?

Please draw or write your thoughts here:

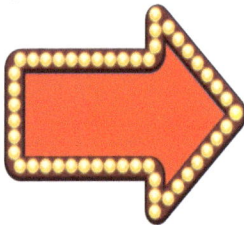

30

AcademyPress ~ http://www.healthyteens.com/

The first day of Nonnie's classes, Alex, Tamika and LaShauna were taking tests. Only Kendle was free to teach. Nonnie introduced her and she led a conversation about respect online.

The class went very well.

After class, Kendle said, "Teaching your peers is different!"

Nonnie nodded. "It is," she said. "In what way?"

Kendle laughed, "They're the same age as me. I worried I might not know more than them, but they listened. I think I taught them something!"

Nonnie agreed.

 AcademyPress ~ http://www.healthyteens.com/

Chapter Seven: David

The next day Nonnie taught her class without peer educators. All the peer educators were busy with school projects!

As she prepared to teach, a wonderful teaching assistant named Mark brought one of his students to her classroom. Mark's job was to spend time with individual students. He worked with young people living with disabilities like Down syndrome.

Mark's student is named David. David had a big smile and was dressed in jeans and a shirt like most of Nonnie's students.

David wanted to attend her classes, just like everyone else.

There was one problem. David's mom didn't want him to attend.

32

     AcademyPress ~ http://www.healthyteens.com/

Nonnie listened to Mark. Then she asked David, "Why do you want to be in my class?"

David said firmly, "I want to learn like everyone else ."

Nonnie asked David, "What do you think the class is about?"

David said quickly, "It's about sex. Right?"

Nonnie smiled. "You're right, David. This year's classes are about consent[6] and using phones and tablets respectfully. Do you have questions?"

David held up his phone. "I have a phone. And I need to know about consent."

Nonnie was pleased. "Great. What do you think consent means?"

David smiled at Mark and then looked at Nonnie. "I think it means to get a 'yes' before you do something. I want to know how to do that." His smile was huge! "I like someone!" he said, and Mark nodded.

Nonnie agreed. David should attend the class. She asked David, "Would you like me to talk with your mom?"

David gave his consent with a huge grin!

[6]See *Nonnie Talks about Consent* for more information

AcademyPress ~ http://www.healthyteens.com/

Nonnie spoke with the school principal. Ms. Keen called David's mother, Ms. Taylor, and arranged a meeting. The three adults met to discuss David attending Nonnie's class.

Nonnie was gentle. "Ms. Taylor, David wants to attend my class," she began.

David's mom said, "I know. I love your class." She gave Nonnie a tiny smile. "You taught me when I was in high school."

Nonnie blushed. "Oh my," she said. "It's nice to be remembered. I guess I am old!"

Everyone laughed loudly. Nonnie noticed. She remembered people often laugh when they're uncomfortable. She thought David's mom felt uneasy. Nonnie said, "May I call you by your first name? It's Sarah, isn't it?"

David's mom grinned. "Of course. You remember me?"

34

AcademyPress ~ http://www.healthyteens.com/

Nonnie said, "Only just now. May I ask you a question?"

When Ms. Taylor said yes, Nonnie asked, "Why do you want to keep David out of class?"

Ms. Taylor was sad, "He'll never need the information. It's not like he'll ever have a real relationship."

Nonnie listened carefully. It sounded like David's mom wanted to protect him. She didn't want him to be hurt. Nonnie asked, "What frightens you?"

Ms. Taylor said, "What if someone touches him and he doesn't want the touch?"

Nonnie thought about how to help Ms. Taylor feel less fearful for her son. She made a few calls and invited Ms. Taylor to meet some of her friends.

She introduced Ms. Taylor to the self-advocates who worked with her on an abuse prevention book for disabled individuals.

Nonnie explained, "Sarah, I believe each person is worthy. Some people with a developmental disability want relationships and some don't, just like everyone else."

 AcademyPress ~ http://www.healthyteens.com/

Ms. Taylor said, "I'll listen to your friends." She joined the self-advocates at their lunch and talked about her son. She shared her fears for him. The self-advocates shared stories about their relationships. When she left, Ms. Taylor said she felt better.

"I'd like David to take your class," she said to Nonnie. "I was wrong. I see what you mean. David may develop a crush or want to have a relationship some day. He needs to understand how his body works."

Nonnie agreed, "Knowing about his body will help. I think all young people need knowledge." She smiled. "I spoke with David. Our theme is how to use phones respectfully and how to give and get consent. David is interested in those topics!"

David was happy to join the class!

Not only was he an interested student, he asked Nonnie if he could teach with her! He asked his mom and she said 'yes'! At the next peer educator training, David began to learn how to teach.

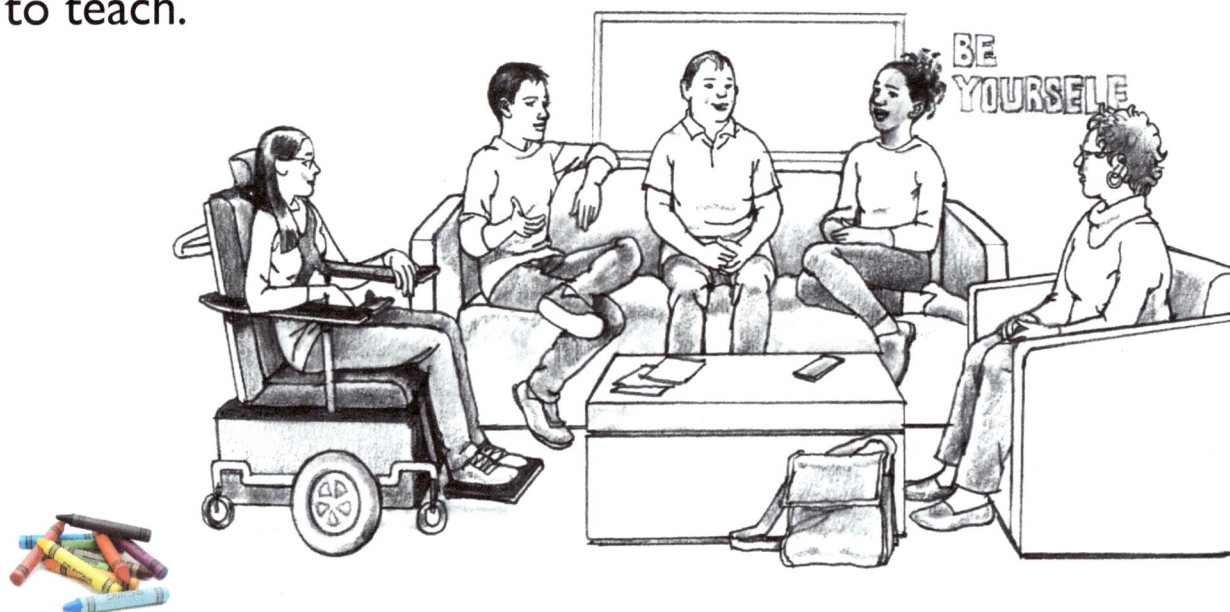

      AcademyPress ~ http://www.healthyteens.com/

He was so very excited!

David wanted to be a good example to his peers.
He learned how to use his phone and tablet respectfully.

Tamika, Alex, and Kendle taught him what to say when he texted with someone. They modeled respectful online behavior.

They all talked about consent and learned how to talk about consent with a partner.

David helped teach his first class. Kendle was there, too.

David became a great role model.

AcademyPress ~ http://www.healthyteens.com/

At the next peer educator meeting, everyone shared the high and low points of their week.

David said, "I loved teaching with Nonnie."

Nonnie grinned. "You did a great job, David," she said.

David sometimes took a little time to say what he was thinking, but he knew exactly what he wanted to say. The others waited until he said, "I liked teaching. I felt good!"

Tamika said, "David, you're using your abilities!"

David's smile was so big it lit up his face!

Kendle said, "We all need to find our best abilities. For me, I love to learn. I love school. I'm smart."

Alex said, "David's physical abilities are strong. He can run and play ball and swim."

David laughed, "You bet I can run! Come to the Special Olympics track meet and watch me!"

The others did see David run!

Alex took a great pic!

AcademyPress ~ http://www.healthyteens.com/

What do YOU Think?

Do you think David could be a good peer educator?
Why or why not?

Everyone has abilities.
Do you know your best ability? What is it?

Please draw
or write your
thoughts
here:

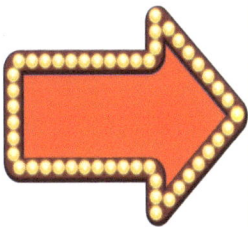

39

AcademyPress ~ http://www.healthyteens.com/

Chapter Eight: Dylan

Nonnie continued teaching. Since David attended her class and became a peer educator, many parents knew Nonnie's classes were inclusive. Inclusive classes make sure as many people as possible are invited into and feel welcome in a space, and there is always room to grow

Not long after David's training, another new student was brought to Nonnie.

The student's name was Dylan. A teacher told Nonnie it might be best if he skipped her class.

The teacher said Dylan doesn't like to sit still in class. He likes to move around the room. Sometimes he even runs around the room. He doesn't always look people in the eye. The teacher said Dylan was an autistic person.

Nonnie thanked the teacher. She'd taught other students like Dylan. She knew Dylan could enjoy class. She just needed to teach the way she always taught—with games and activities! For Dylan, these games and activities made learning more assessible.

40

AcademyPress ~ http://www.healthyteens.com/

Most students love to move. Dylan needed to move! He also needed protected from bright lights and loud, sudden noises.

Nonnie decided to meet with Dylan before class.

She asked his parents to bring him to her office. She bought some crunchy apples in case he was hungry. Nonnie wanted to prepare a learning space that would make learning accessible for Dylan.

Nonnie could tell right away that Dylan was a smart young person!

He told her all about his family trip to Disney World! He really liked Toy Story Land! He likes to take pictures just like Alex. He took great pics at Disney.

Dylan talked most about how much he loved his family.

When Nonnie asked him if he wanted to go to her class, Dylan said, "Yes, please!"

41

Dylan's parents were happy he'd be included in Nonnie's class.

They asked Nonnie if she would meet with Dylan's sisters. They were caring parents and wanted to know if the girls were happy.

Nonnie met with Dylan's sisters in the park beside her office.

One of his sisters is named Melody. She's 12. Dylan's other sister is named Rebecca. She's 8 years old.

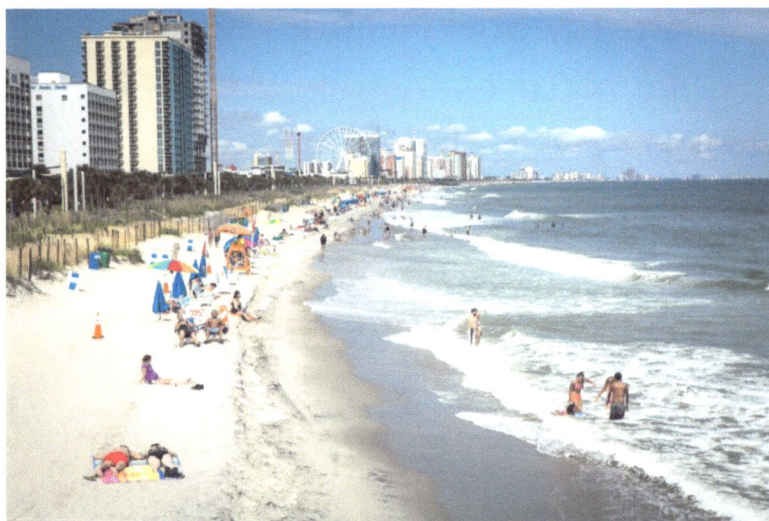

The girls were open and talked honestly about their brother. It was easy to see they loved him. They shared family fun, like going to the beach and playing in the sand and ocean.

AcademyPress ~ http://www.healthyteens.com/

They talked about their love for Halloween. This year Dylan wanted to be a skeleton! They talked about how much they loved their brother.

Then, Nonnie asked if there were times when it was hard to be Dylan's sister

The girls waited a moment.

Nonnie said, "I believe you love your brother. It's OK to be honest."

Melody said, "I get annoyed at him at times."

Rebecca said, "Me too."

Both girls looked troubled, as if they shouldn't share their feelings.

Nonnie asked, "Are the two of you ever annoyed with each other?"

The sisters looked at each other and burst into laughter.

Nonnie smiled, "People who love each other don't get along all the time! Your feelings are OK."

43

AcademyPress ~ http://www.healthyteens.com/

Melody thought a moment, then she said, "It's embarrassing if Dylan interrupts others when they're talking."

Nonnie nodded, "Of course."

Melody added quickly, "I love him even if I'm annoyed."

Rebecca said, "I don't like it when he plays with my toys and doesn't leave me alone when my friends come over."

Then Rebecca said, "I still love him lots!"

Nonnie listened carefully to Dylan's sisters.

"What other things about living with your brother can be difficult?" she asked gently.

Melody was quiet.

Rebecca said, "We play together pretty well. Sometimes Dylan can be bossy. Like when we're making up things, and he wants to talk about something over and over."

Nonnie thought the girls looked guilty.

She repeated what she said earlier. "Your feelings are important. It's OK to share them."

44

    AcademyPress ~ http://www.healthyteens.com/

Rebecca said, "Dylan has feelings, too."

Nonnie agreed. "Do you think he might feel left out at times?"

Rebecca nodded.

Melody sighed, "What bothers me the most are boundaries. It's tough for Dylan to understand boundaries."

Nonnie asked, "Can you explain what the word boundary means to you?

"That's easy, Nonnie," Melody said.

"My friend Mindy asked me to take a pic of her at school. We were talking about boundaries in class. Mindy drew this chalk line around her to show her own space."

Nonnie nodded. "Yes. Everyone needs to feel safe. How does Dylan misunderstand boundaries?

Melody said, "Like when my friends are over to hang out and he won't leave us alone. Or when I want to read quietly or text my friends and he keeps talking to me about the same thing over and over."

 AcademyPress ~ http://www.healthyteens.com/

Nonnie said, "What helps?"

Both girls answered so fast, Nonnie smiled.

"Including him as much as we can," Rebecca said.

Melody agreed. "We each do our own activities and spend time with our parents alone.

Rebecca added, "And our parents listen to how we feel."

Nonnie asked, "How do your parents help when you're all together and Dylan doesn't understand boundaries?"

The girls talked quietly to each other, then Melody said, "They usually distract him with something."

Rebecca nodded. "He really likes to cook," she said.

Melody laughed. "Mostly he likes to bake." Melody is like Alex and David; she likes to take pictures. She shared this one with Nonnie.

Rebecca licked her lips. "He makes great cupcakes!" she said.

Nonnie was pleased.

She could see all three siblings were respected and heard.

    AcademyPress ~ http://www.healthyteens.com/

What do YOU Think?

Why do you think the teacher told Nonnie it would be best if Dylan didn't attend her class?

Pretend you're a teacher. Do you think some of your students will like school more than others? Do you think some students may *need* to move like Dylan? How would you respect those students and help them love learning?

Please draw or write your thoughts here:

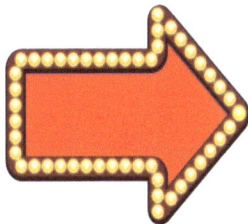

47

AcademyPress ~ http://www.healthyteens.com/

Nonnie understood why Rebecca and Melody's parents wanted her to talk with the girls. They wanted to be sure they were doing the right thing.

Melody decided to be a peer educator and Rebecca said she'd like to teach with Nonnie when she was older.

They asked Dylan if he wanted to teach. He said 'no', then 'maybe', and then started to hang out at peer educator meetings.

Everyone is different!

When Melody started coming to the Teen Center, she shared her brother's interest in art. Dylan was talented. He could make just about anything out of paper, tape and markers!

Tamika and Alex were interested. They invited Dylan to the Teen Center's art room. They discovered his sister was right! Dylan was very creative.

 AcademyPress ~ http://www.healthyteens.com/

Chapter Nine: Malik

Alex called Nonnie at home to share their time with Dylan.

Alex said, "Dylan has a lot of abilities, Nonnie. His abilities are important, just like David's and Kendle's abilities are important.

Nonnie was pleased. "Just like Tamika and your abilities are important. They're just all unique."

Alex said, "Can you imagine if we were all the same? Each person is worthy." Nonnie was proud of her grandson Alex. She wondered if he could tell how big her smile was over the phone.

Later that week, Nonnie was preparing for class when a sign language interpreter named Ms. Luciana came to see her. Ms. Luciana said she was working with a student named Malik. Malik is Deaf. Ms. Luciana asked if she could attend Nonnie's class and interpret for Malik. Nonnie said, "Sure!"

AcademyPress ~ http://www.healthyteens.com/

Malik did very well in Nonnie's class. He was able to follow along because Ms. Luciana signed everything Nonnie said.

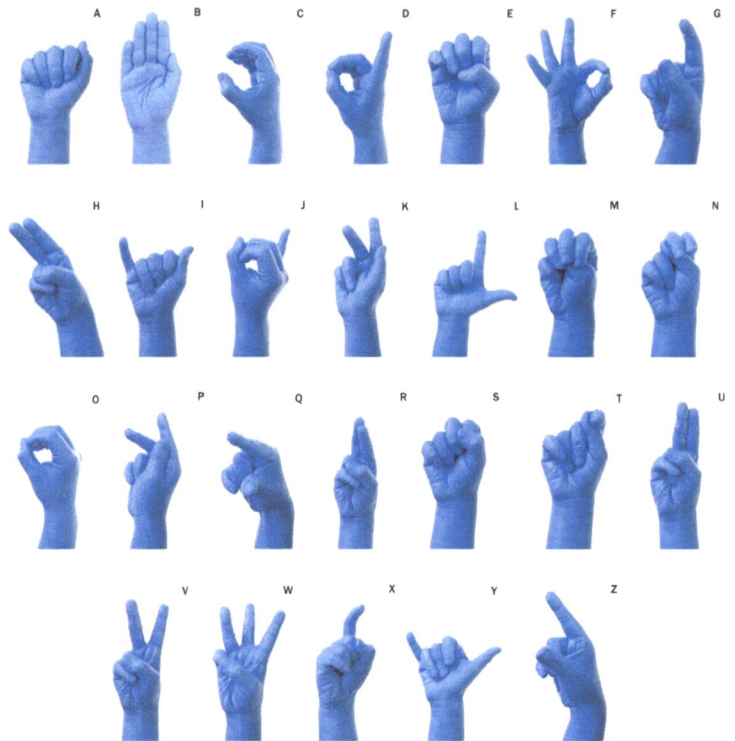

Nonnie knew to speak slowly so Ms. Luciana could follow her words and interpret them for Malik. She also knew how important it was to ask Malik how he wanted to communicate. She wanted to respect Malik as she respected all her students.

Nonnie felt badly. She wanted to speak directly to Malik without an interpreter. She asked him for suggestions.

Malik showed her how to say a few things by signing. He told her about an American Sign Language (ASL) class at the library.

Nonnie went to the class that weekend and every Saturday for weeks. She called a professor friend whose daughter was Deaf and he helped her study.

She learned how to sign, "I'm happy you're in my class," to Malik.

AcademyPress ~ http://www.healthyteens.com/

Malik smiled. He signed "Thank you," by putting his flat hand against his lips and moving it towards Nonnie.

Nonnie was happy! She understood learning ASL was like learning any language. The more she used the language, the more it would be part of her life!

Malik was patient. He showed her how to sign many words and phrases. He was a good teacher!

Nonnie was thrilled!

The next peer educator meeting, Nonnie talked about her decision to continue sign language classes. She wanted to be able to speak with Malik and other Deaf students.

Kendle said, "Malik has lots of abilities, Nonnie. He's a good student and likes to draw. Maybe one of his best abilities is teaching you a new language!"

Nonnie agreed. Teaching others is a great ability!

Malik began hanging out at the Teen Center. He fit right in with the other teens. He took a pic with his new phone!

 AcademyPress ~ http://www.healthyteens.com/

Malik taught the peer educators signing whenever they asked him to sign words.

He was very busy with school and activities, so there was no time for him to train to be a peer educator yet, but he promised to help at the Center. The peer educators discovered he played basketball and started following his team.

They told Nonnie the next time she was at the Center. She said, "That makes sense. I'm not much of an athlete, but I do know basketball is a sport with a lot of body language."

Tamika asked, "How is body language important in basketball?"

Malik knows lipreading, which means he can 'read' what people are saying by watching their lips, their gestures, and their movements. He answered Tamika. "You need to play basketball by watching all the players and the ref and the ball," he said. "And figuring out where the ball will probably go next."

Alex shook his head. "Isn't that hard?" he asked. Alex was practicing signing and he tried to sign the question.

Malik grinned, then helped Alex sign correctly. He said, "It's not hard at all. It's just fun!"

David said, "See. Everyone's abilities are good!"

AcademyPress ~ http://www.healthyteens.com/

![WHAT DO YOU THINK?]

What do YOU Think?

Nonnie wanted to sign with Malik. Would you like to learn sign language (ASL)? Why or why not?

Some people think everyone should learn to sign because it is a language everyone can understand.
What do you think?

Please draw or write your thoughts here:

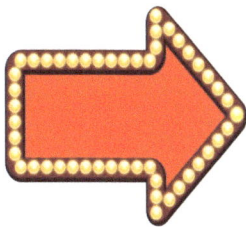

AcademyPress ~ http://www.healthyteens.com/

Chapter Ten: Relationships

Alex and Kendle were working together on a new activity for their classes. They were planning a parent workshop where they would be part of a panel. They were excited and ready to go!

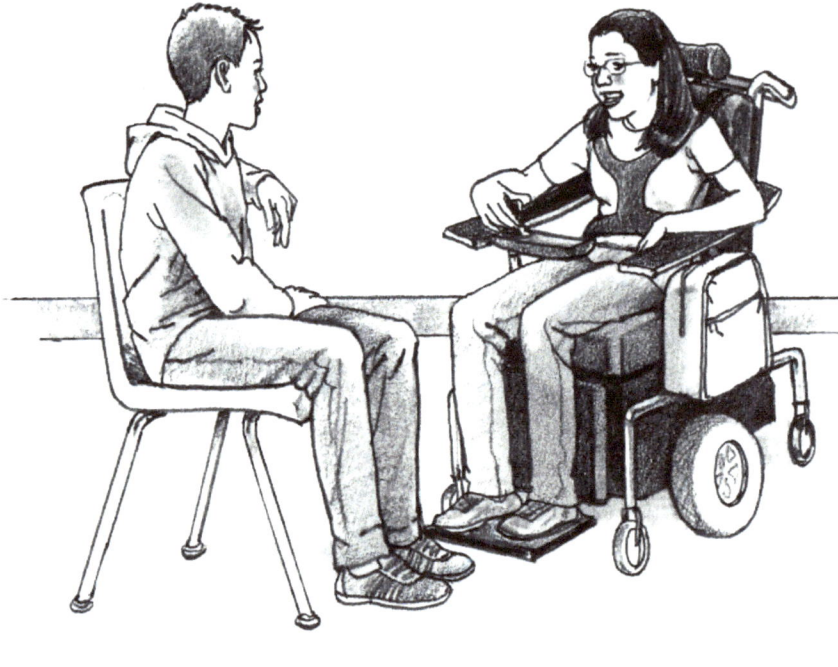

Nonnie watched. She heard their laughter and it made her smile.

Nonnie knew one of the best parts of peer education was the way young people meet their peers and learn to work together. Sometimes, those young people become friends. Other times, those young people become more than friends and *really* like each other!

Nonnie asked Alex and Kendle to research the kinds of disabilities people may live with so they could be aware of them and learn to respect each person.[7]

She stepped back to let them work.

[7]Alex and Kendle's Research is in Appendix 1 on pages 66 and 67

 AcademyPress ~ http://www.healthyteens.com/

English Braille Alphabet

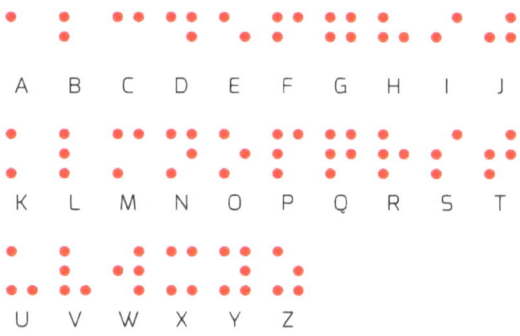

A B C D E F G H I J
K L M N O P Q R S T
U V W X Y Z

Kendle said, "I think we should be more aware of those who cannot see or have difficulty seeing. There should be more braille books at the library, so people can read through touch."

Alex said, "That's a great idea! Braille books use raised dots to make letters so they can be touched instead of seen. What about invisible disabilities? How can we support everyone?"

Kendle said, "I'm happy you're starting to think about ability privilege, Alex. You're a good ally and accomplice."

Alex thought she looked sad. He said, "I'm missing something, aren't I?"

Kendle just smiled.

Alex was suddenly anxious. He didn't know what to say to make Kendle feel better. He wanted her to be happy.

anxious

Alex thought—what would Nonnie say? He remembered Nonnie's lessons about empathy. Stop thinking of yourself, Alex, he thought.

Alex said, "Kendle, I like working with you. Please know you can say anything to me. Anything at all."

55

AcademyPress ~ http://www.healthyteens.com/

Kendle sighed. "It's great to respect disabled people Alex, but ableism still makes most people see us as different."

Alex was confused. "We're all different," he said.

Kendle nodded. "But no one ever pats you on the head and acts like you're still a little kid."

Alex was shocked. "People do that?"

Kendle said, "Not often, but sometimes. People with disabilities can also be treated like they're always good. Everyone makes mistakes."

Alex snorted. "I'd never treat you like that!" Then he said with a grin. "I know you're not perfect!"

Kendle gave him a tiny smile and added, "It's not right when people without disabilities make decisions for disabled people. And, I really hate it when a person talks to someone I'm with instead of me. Like I'm not there. Or when they assume things about me."

Alex leaned closer. He was interested and a little angry. Kendle was his friend and he didn't want people treating her badly. "Tell me more." he said gently. "What do they assume?"

Kendle was quiet a moment, and then she said quickly. "Like they assume I won't get accepted by a good college. Or get a good job."

     AcademyPress ~ http://www.healthyteens.com/

Alex was shocked. He said, "Kendle, you're the smartest kid in our grade. You're already taking an AP class. I know you'll get into college. You'll get a good job, too."

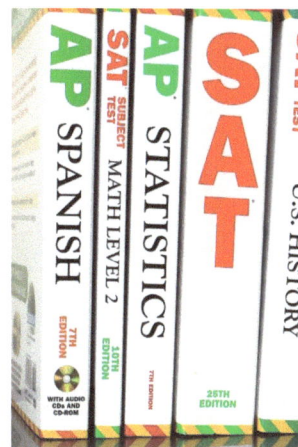

Kendle was quiet. Alex said, "I feel like something else is bothering you, Kendle."

Kendle took a deep breath. "It's how I think some people see me. It's as if they assume I'll never have a partner? I want to."

Alex was confused. "A partner like someone to help open a store or create a business?

Kendle giggled, "No silly. Not that kind of partner. A romantic partner."

Alex gasped. "Oh yeah," he said, feeling foolish.

Kendle said, "I know people wonder if I'll ever get married. I don't mind that as much as…" When Kendle stopped talking, Alex encouraged, "as much as…."

Kendle blushed. "I think people might think I'm not sexy."

Alex said, "But you are!"

Now Alex blushed, which made Kendle laugh. "I'm not laughing at you, Alex," she said. "I'm laughing at both of us."

AcademyPress ~ http://www.healthyteens.com/

Alex mumbled, "Talking about sexy stuff is weird."

Both Alex and Kendle laughed. Nonnie listened, but didn't speak. She wanted them to work out their discomfort.

Alex finally said, "I'm glad you were brave and told me."

Kendle grinned. "You're a good listener and I know you respect me."

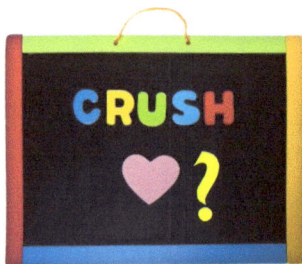

Alex couldn't find the words he wanted to say. Did he like Kendle? *Really* like her?

Kendle said, "Let's get back to our assignment. What can we all do to make others feel respected?" she asked.

Alex added, "And worthy."

Kendle said, "One easy thing we can do is be careful with our words."

Alex agreed. "Words matter."

Kendle nodded. "There are hurtful words people use—sometimes without even thinking–that act as if people living with disabilities aren't equal or even human."

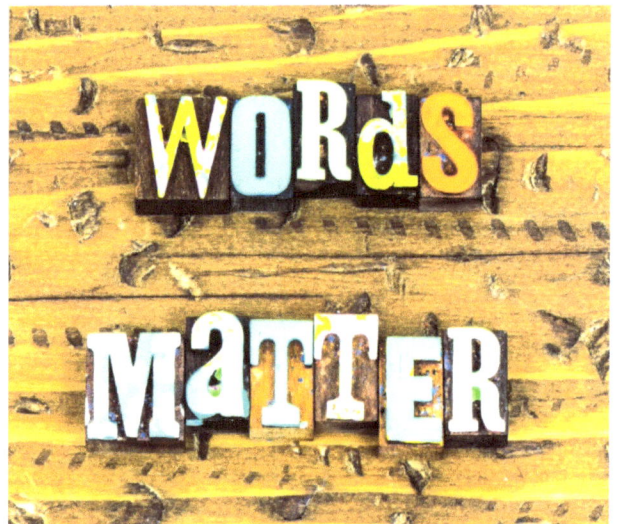

Alex frowned. "I'd never say those words," he said.

AcademyPress ~ http://www.healthyteens.com/

What do YOU Think?

What do YOU Think?

Kendle and Alex started talking about difficult topics. Would this be a courageous conversation?

Why do you think some people treat disabled people as if they are small children or aren't sexy?
How do you think that kind of treatment would feel?

Please draw or write your thoughts here:

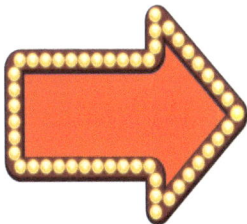

59

AcademyPress ~ http://www.healthyteens.com/

Chapter Eleven: Bystanders and Bullying

Kendle turned to Nonnie. She said, "How did you teach Alex to speak with respect?"

Alex answered for Nonnie. "When I was little, she told me the rhyme 'Sticks and stones will break my bones but words will never hurt me' is a lie!"

Nonnie was pleased. "Why do you think it's a lie?" she asked.

"Because words CAN hurt." Alex said confidently.

Kendle liked the way Alex spoke. She asked, "What would you do if you heard someone else saying hurtful words?"

Alex was quiet as he thought about Kendle's question. Then, he asked, "Nonnie, wouldn't that be bullying?"

Nonnie said, "It would. Young people living with disabilities are often bullied because of their disabilities."

Alex said, "I know what I should do. I should step up and stop those kinds of words from being used." He paused. "What would I say?"

AcademyPress ~ http://www.healthyteens.com/

Tamika and David came into the room. They were in the art room working on guideline cards for their class. They heard Nonnie's question.

David said, "I would say, "Stop that right now!"

Tamika said, "I would speak up if I heard someone using a hurtful word."

Alex took a deep breath and said, "I would say—*Using hurtful words isn't OK. Please stop.*" Kendle smiled at her friend.

Nonnie loved the way the peer educators talked about hurtful words. She told them she was pleased and then said, "Does anyone know the meaning of the word bystander?"

The peer educators looked at each other. They shook their heads no.

Alex guessed, "Someone standing beside someone else?"

"Close," said Nonnie. "Bystanders are people who are nearby when a person is bullied or hurt."

Tamika asked, "Why is this important, Nonnie?"

Nonnie said, "If bystanders speak up, they offer support."

 AcademyPress ~ http://www.healthyteens.com/

What do YOU Think?

Have you heard people say hurtful words to a person living with a disability? Are you a bystander?

Do you think you should speak up?
What would you say or do to stop this type of bullying?

Please draw or write your thoughts here:

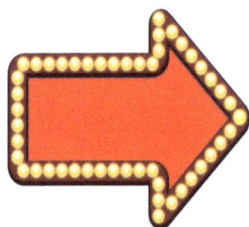

AcademyPress ~ http://www.healthyteens.com/

Kendle said, "Maybe the bullying will stop."

Tamika agreed and added, "Maybe that's the best part of learning to be a peer educator. We can be people who aren't afraid to stand with anyone who needs support."

They all thought about courage. Sometimes being brave was more than just courageous conversations!

They talked about ableism and accessibility. They shared their experiences and reminded themselves what they'd learned.

Are you BRAVE?

They discovered how to make spaces more inclusive and welcoming.

They learned how important accessible ramps and elevators could be. They learned some learning spaces were not safe for people living with a physical disability.

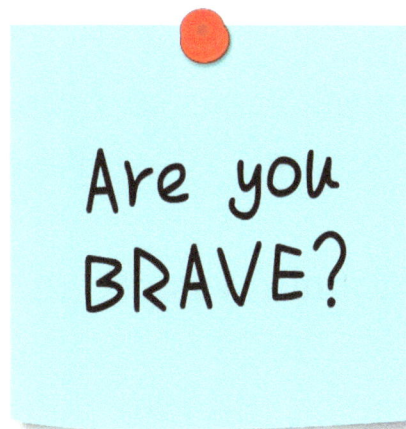

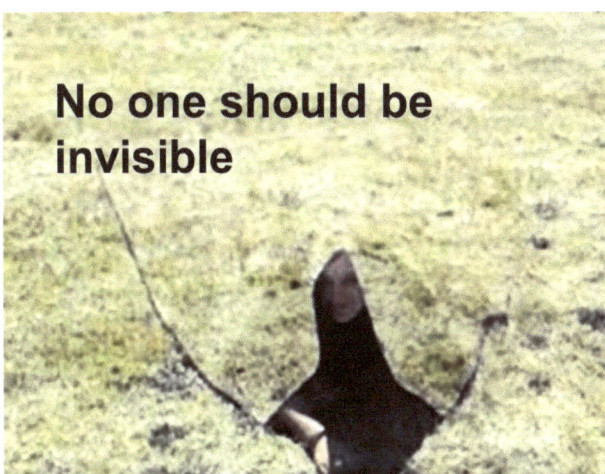

No one should be invisible

They began to understand that learning spaces for autistic or developmentally disabled students needed to be places where it was easier for those students to learn.

They now knew no one should be made to feel invisible.

 AcademyPress ~ http://www.healthyteens.com/

Kendle added, "Remember, people with disabilities are all different. If you've met *one* person with a disability, you've met *one* person with a disability!"

Alex and Tamika exchanged looks.

Tamika said to Nonnie, "We learned a lot during peer educator training!" Alex agreed.

Nonnie was proud.

Finally, the peer educators were finished with their training. It was time for them to teach without Nonnie's help. Some of the new peer educators taught together. They started class with guidelines and promises.

They did a great job.

AcademyPress ~ http://www.healthyteens.com/

What do YOU Think?

This book talked about disability.

How has it changed the way you think about disability?

How can you be more respectful to others in your life?

Please draw
or write your
thoughts
here:

AcademyPress ~ http://www.healthyteens.com/

Appendix 1: (Alex and Kendle's Research)

Alex and Kendle researched the types of disability they encountered as they learned. They want to share their new knowledge!

Autism or Autism Spectrum Disorder: The Autism Self Advocacy Network (ASAN https://autisticadvocacy.org/) discusses autism or autism spectrum disorder in this way: "Autism is a neurological variation that occurs in about one percent of the population and is classified as a developmental disability. While all Autistics are as unique as any other human beings, they share some characteristics typical of autism in common.
1. Different sensory experiences.
2. Non-standard ways of learning and approaching problem solving.
3. Deeply focused thinking and passionate interests in specific subjects.
4. Atypical, sometimes repetitive, movement.
5. Need for consistency, routine, and order.
6. Difficulties in understanding and expressing language as used in typical communication, both verbal and non-verbal.
7. Difficulties in understanding and expressing typical social interaction."

ASAN, like other disability advocacy groups, uses the phrase "Nothing about us without us," to underscore that self-advocates' voices need to be heard. Self-advocates must be part of any decision affecting their own health and well-being. "Nothing about us without us" is a good way to think about interacting and respecting any disabled person. The book character Dylan represents a young autistic person.

Deaf: According to the National Association of the Deaf (https://www.nad.org/) individuals refer to themselves in any way they feel comfortable. Typically a lowercase deaf refers to the audiological condition of not hearing, and the uppercase Deaf refers to a particular group of deaf people who share a language – American Sign Language (ASL) – and a culture. If a person uses lipreading to communicate, the speaker should face the person directly, face into the light, and keep hands or other items away from the mouth. The book character Malik represents a Deaf teen.

Developmental Disability: The Arc (https://thearc.org/) is an organization advocating for individuals with intellectual and developmental disabilities. Their Position Statement on Self-Advocacy can be found at https://thearc.org/position-statements/self-advocacy/. The Statement contains policies on independence, voting, leadership, and other human rights.

Down Syndrome: In every cell in the human body there is a nucleus, where genetic material is stored in genes. Genes carry the codes responsible for all of our inherited traits and are grouped along rod-like structures called chromosomes. Typically, the nucleus of each cell contains 23 pairs of chromosomes, half of which are inherited from each parent. Down syndrome occurs when an individual has a full or partial extra copy of chromosome 21.

AcademyPress ~ http://www.healthyteens.com/

Appendix 1: Continued

This additional genetic material alters the course of development and causes the characteristics associated with Down syndrome. A few of the common physical traits of Down syndrome are low muscle tone, small stature, an upward slant to the eyes, and a single deep crease across the center of the palm – although each person with Down syndrome is a unique individual and may possess these characteristics to different degrees, or not at all. (National Down Syndrome Society definition—https://www.ndss.org/). The character David in the book represents a young person living with Down Syndrome.

Physical Disability: There are many types of physical disabilities. Kendle's disability represents one type. She lives with a type of muscular dystrophy. Please see the (Muscular Dystrophy Association-https://www.mda.org/). There are nine types of muscular dystrophies, which are categorized as neuromuscular disorders. They are genetic, degenerative diseases primarily affecting voluntary muscles. Each type is different.

Respecting all people means learning about their lives and developing empathy for their experiences.

There are many types of physical disabilities. Here are a few:

- **Cerebral Palsy:** Cerebral palsy (CP) is a problem that affects muscle tone, movement, and motor skills. CP often is caused by brain damage that happens before or during a baby's birth, or during the first 3-to-5 years of a child's life. (United Cerebral Palsy Foundation https://ucp.org/).

- **Multiple Sclerosis:** Multiple sclerosis (MS) is an unpredictable disease of the central nervous system that disrupts the flow of information within the brain, and between the brain and body. (National Multiple Sclerosis Society—https://www.nationalmssociety.org/What-is-MS).

- **Spinal Cord Injury:** People with a spinal cord injury (SCI) have experienced damage to any part of the spinal cord or nerves at the end of the spinal canal (cauda equina). This injury often causes permanent changes in strength, sensation and other body functions below the site of the injury. Christopher Reeve, the actor who played Superman, and his wife Dana created a Foundation to assist with self-advocacy and provide recourses for those living with a SCI after Mr. Reeve was paralyzed from a fall. (Christopher and Dana Reeve Foundation https://www.christopherreeve.org/)

As LaShauna said, we need to learn about disabilities, listen to self-advocates and treat others with respect.

Please find a wonderful guide to disability etiquette here: https://ucp.org/resource-guide/

AcademyPress ~ http://www.healthyteens.com/

Appendix 2: Food for Thought

Author's Note:

Writing *Nonnie Talks about Disability* was a true learning experience for me. My first and best decision was to ask Kendle to be my consulting author for the book. We began the book in the fall of 2018, but I was diagnosed with breast cancer in December. Surgery, recover and chemo made me put the book aside. I'm really pleased with the result, and would like to share four areas where I think need more discussion is needed. I write this for adults, but I would expect adults to share with their young people, depending on their developmental readiness for these concepts.

Person-First-Language: I was taught to use person-first-language (PFL) or person-centered language in both my nursing and counseling trainings. An example of PFL would be, "Mr. S is living with diabetes". The person is said first; the person is more important than the disease or challenge in the person's life. However, in talking with self-advocates, I discovered some people with disabilities do NOT like this way of being discussed. Self-advocates told me, for example, that being a person on the autism spectrum is not a disease or something they want to remove. It is part of them. Following their lead, I introduce the character Dylan as an autistic person on page 40. Dylan's character lives with autism but does not need to be different than he is—he is an autistic person. The same is true for the term disabled persons. It's vital to listen to people; no one should decide how a person wants to be described.

Neurotypical: One definition of the term neurotypical describes those individuals who do not have a diagnosis of autism or any other intellectual or developmental difference. A "neurotypical" person seen as an individual who thinks, perceives, and behaves in ways that are considered to be "normal" by the general population. Normal is defined by those in power. Our young people joke that normal is a setting on a clothes dryer. The truth is, each person is a person of worth. Referring to any person as not *normal* is degrading and denies worth.

The R-word: I address hurtful words on pages 58-62. Our peer educators regularly sponsor a campaign to remove the R-Word from conversation.

   AcademyPress ~ http://www.healthyteens.com/

Appendix 3: Some World Religions

There are many world religions. These are symbols of a few major religious groups and religions, from left to right: Christianity, Islam, Hinduism, Buddhism, Taoism, Shinto, Sikhism, Judaism and Baha'i.

A short explanation of each religion is:

Baha'i: The Bahá'í Faith has three core assertions, sometimes termed the "three onenesses", that are central in the teachings of the religion. They are the Oneness of God, the Oneness of Religion and the Oneness of Humanity. They also referred to as the unity of God, of religion, and of mankind.

Buddhism: A religion of eastern and central Asia growing out of the teaching of Siddhārtha Gautama stressing that suffering is inherent in life and that one can be liberated from it by cultivating wisdom, virtue, and concentration.

Christianity: The religion derived from Jesus Christ, based on the Bible as sacred scripture, and professed by Eastern, Roman Catholic, and Protestant groups. Two firm commandments for behavior as a Christian are "You shall love the Lord thy God with all your heart, and with all your soul, and with all your mind. This is the first and great commandment. And the second is like it, you shalt love your neighbor as your self". (Mark 12: 28-34)

Judaism: A monotheistic religion developed among the ancient Hebrews. Judaism is characterized by a belief in one transcendent God who revealed himself to Abraham, Moses, and the Hebrew prophets and by a religious life in accordance with Scriptures and rabbinic traditions.

Hinduism: The dominant religion of India that emphasizes dharma (the right way of living), with its resulting ritual/social observances and often mystical contemplation and ascetic practice.

Islam: Is an Arabic word meaning "submission" and means "submission to the will of God". The religion of the Muslims, a monotheistic faith regarded as revealed through Muhammad as the Prophet of Allah. Islam seeks complete peace through submission to the will of Allah.

Shinto: A Japanese religion dating from the early 8th century and incorporating the worship of ancestors and nature spirits with a belief in sacred power (*kami*) in both animate and inanimate things. It was the state religion of Japan until 1945.

Sikhism: A monotheistic, monist, pantheist religion that originated in the 15th century from the Punjab region in the Indian subcontinent. The term "Sikh" means disciple, student.

Taoism: A Chinese philosophy based on the writings of Lao-tzu and advocating humility and religious piety. Taoism tends to emphasize naturalness, spontaneity, simplicity, detachment

AcademyPress ~ http://www.healthyteens.com/

Glossary

Ableism: Discrimination or prejudice against people living with disabilities.

Accessible Ramp: A ramp or slopped entry way built to allow people using wheelchairs or canes or other devices easier access (entry) into areas where stairs or uneven flooring is standard.

Accessibility: A term describing parts of life which influence a person's ability to interact with the environment. It can refer to the measure of how simply and easily a person can participate in life.

Accomplice: In human rights work, an accomplice is not someone who contributes to a crime, but rather someone who works to dismantle systems that are unjust. Accomplices are committed to cooperation and community.

Advantages: Situations that put a person in a favorable position.

Ageism: Prejudice or discrimination due to a person's age.

Ally: A person who is a member of a dominant or majority group who stands with those who are minorities to remove oppression.

American Sign Language (ASL): A visual language based on a naturally evolved system of hand gestures and their placement relative to the body, along with non-manual markers such as facial expressions, head movements, shoulder raises, and movements of the body.

Annoyed: A little irritated or angry.

Anti-Semitism: Hostility or prejudice against Jews.

Anxious: Feeling worry, unease, or nervousness.

AP class: An advanced placement class where students are challenged with more difficult material.

Assume: When someone supposes something to be the case, without proof.

Autistic Person: A person living with autism, or autism spectrum disorder (ASD), refers to a broad range of conditions characterized by challenges with social skills, repetitive behaviors, speech and nonverbal communication. Please see page 65 for a discussion on person centered language.

Glossary

Aware: Having knowledge or perception of a fact; being concerned about.

Blushed: Developing a pink coloring in the face from embarrassment.

Body Language: The gestures, movements and mannerisms people use to communicate with others.

Boundary: A line that defines the end of or beginning of an area. With personal space, the line where a person feels comfortable with touch or nearness. With consent, a limit a person chooses for behavior or contact with another.

Braille: A system of writing for Blind people that uses characters made up of raised dots for letters.

Buddhist Temple: A place of worship for Buddhists (followers of Buddhism).

Bullying: A person is being bullied with he or she is exposed, repeatedly and over time, to negative actions on part of one or more persons (Olweus, 1993*)

Bystander: Those who witness something like bullying. A bystander is passive when no response is made to the bullying.

Challenges: Events or situations that are complicated or difficult and require an effort to get through.

Christian: A follower of Jesus Christ. A believer in Christianity's principles.

Cisgender: A person who identifies as the sex assigned at birth by body parts.

Complicated: Not simple.

Confidence: A feeling or belief that a person can do something and succeed.

Consent: Permission for something to happen or agreeing to do something.

Courageous Conversations: The courage to have the type of conversation about difficult topics that is positive and leads to progress.

Cultures: The ways of life for a group of people—how they do things. Young people's culture is not the same as the culture of adults.

*As defined by the Olweus Bullying Prevention Program (OBPP). Dr. Podgurski is a certified OBPP trainer.

AcademyPress ~ http://www.healthyteens.com/

Glossary

Depression: A common mental illness causing feelings of sadness and loss of interest in activities. Depression is treatable.

Determined: Having made a decision and deciding not to change it.

Disability: A person with a disability is a person who has a physical or mental impairment that substantially limits one or more major life activity. (ADA—American Disability Association definition).

Discussion Leaders: People trained to lead or facilitate conversation.

Down Syndrome: A common birth defect that is usually due to an extra chromosome 21(trisomy 21) See page 65 for a deeper definition.

Embarrassed: A feeling as if a person is being awkward or judged or exposed.

Empathy: The act of understanding, being aware of, being sensitive to, and vicariously experiencing the feelings, thoughts, and experience of another.

Engaged: Connected. In education, students are engaged when they are participating and involved in activities to enhance understanding.

Ethnicity: A social group that shares the same background or heritage.

Facilitators: Those trained to make discussion or dialogue easy.

Gender: Refers to the socially constructed characteristics of women and men – such as norms, roles and relationships of and between groups of women and men. It varies from society to society and can be changed. (World Health Organization definition).

Heterosexual: Someone attracted romantically, emotionally or sexually to people of a different sex or gender to self. One type of sexual orientation. Also called straight.

Immigrated: Moved from one country to another.

Inclusive: Accepting to all types of people. In education, a commitment to provide learning spaces where all students can learn and grow.

Individual: A person. One human.

AcademyPress ~ http://www.healthyteens.com/

Glossary

Invisible: Not seen. If a person says they 'feel invisible' they often mean they feel ignored or unseen.

Inspire: Give someone the urge to do something, especially something creative.

Isms: A philosophy, which may be political. In this context, the term isms refers to stereotypes perpetuated against groups of people.

Jewish: Refers to both those who follow the ethnoreligious beliefs of Judaism and to the those who are from a group descended from the Israelites.

Learning Disability: A disorder in one or more basic psychological processes that may manifest itself as an imperfect ability in certain areas of learning, such as reading, written expression, or mathematics (ALDA—Learning Disability Association of America definition)

Lipreading: Lip reading allows a person to "listen" to a speaker by watching the speaker's face to figure out their speech patterns, movements, gestures and expressions. Some Deaf people use lipreading along with ASL.

Megaphone: A cone shaped device used to magnify the voice.

Mental Health Diagnosis: When a health care professional accesses a person and finds a mental illness. Mental illnesses are health conditions involving changes in emotion, thinking or behavior (or a combination of these) (American Psychiatric Association Definition).

Mission: In this context, a statement of a group's core purpose or reason for the work that is done.

Misunderstand: Failure to 'get' or understand something correctly.

Mocked: Made fun of, laughed at—to be treated with ridicule and contempt.

Mosque: A Muslim place of worship.

Naples: A city in southern Italy. Naples is a SW port and the third largest city in the country.

Partner: In this context, a person with whom one is connected romantically or sexually. May also mean a person with whom one does business.

AcademyPress ~ http://www.healthyteens.com/

Glossary

Peer Educators: Young people trained to teach their peers.

Peers: People the same age.

Perspective: How one sees things. Point of view.

Privilege: A special right, advantage, or immunity granted or available only to a particular person or group.

"Privilege means not having to think about something": One way to look at privilege. In this book, the peer educators didn't even think of how Kendle would get into the teaching space.

Race: A concept that defines humans into groups based on characteristics or biological traits.

Racism: The belief in the superiority of one race over another. It may also mean prejudice, discrimination, or antagonism directed against other people because they are of a different race or ethnicity.

Research: Looking at a topic and examining it through study.

Respect Online: Part of Dr. Podgurski's Peer Educator Program where older teens teach middle school students how to avoid cyberbullying online while respecting themselves, their bodies, and the feelings and bodies of others.

Respectful Online Behavior: Behavior where each person using social media or texting treats others with respect.

Role Models; Individuals who model positive behavior for others.

Romantic: Connected to love or an expression of love.

Self-advocates: People who understands their strengths and weaknesses, develops personal goals, and is assertive (which means standing up for oneself), and making decisions. The verb advocate is part of the peer educator mission statement and means to support.

Self-conscious: Feeling uncomfortable, embarrassed or nervous when with other people; feeling as if a person is being judged or observed.

AcademyPress ~ http://www.healthyteens.com/

Glossary

Self-worth: The opinion a person holds of self; the value a person places on self. Dr. Podgurski believes each person is a person of worth.

Sexual Orientation: Patterns of sexual, romantic or emotional attraction to others and one's identity based on those attractions.

Sexy: Feeling sexually attractive or being seen as sexually attractive. In this context. Part of ableism is the failure to see those living with disability as sexually attractive humans with sexual needs.

Sibling: Children in the same family.

Sign Language Interpreter: An individual trained in ASL or another sign language who translates spoken word into signing.

Stereotypes: A fixed idea of a group of people that may be untrue or only partly true.

Swear Words: Words seen as unacceptable. Also known as 'cuss words'. Each culture has their own words deemed as swear words.

Teachable Moment: A time when education is possible, typically outside a formal classroom.

Teaching Assistant: In this context, someone who works—often one and one—with individuals who need assistance learning.

Topic: A subject for conversation or discussion.

Trusted Adults: Adults who respect and care for young people.

Uneasy: Feeling uncomfortable or awkward.

Unique: One of a kind. Each person is unique.

White Privilege: Advantages possessed by a white person on the basis of their race in a society characterized by racial inequality and injustice. It exists because of enduring racism and bias.

Worthy: When a person is seen as praiseworthy, having value.

Endorsements

Nonnie Talks about Disability is the ninth volume in the interactive Nonnie Talks series. As with each of the topics in Dr. Mary Jo Podgurski's previous books, Nonnie introduces the subject of disability with respect and compassionate regard for the needs of self and others.

The story begins with the relatable experience of a young child asking an ill-timed question about a person in a wheelchair. Nonnie uses the "teachable moment" to help both adult and child readers to understand that people have many kinds of differences that create challenges, as well as opportunities and gifts.

Through her wide lens of experience as a pediatric oncology nurse, counselor, educator, advocate, parent and grandparent, Dr. Mary Jo Podgurski is a credible voice for the dignity and respect of all individuals.

Nonnie Talks About Disability provides a vehicle to open the dialogue between children and their trusted caregivers in a respectful and non-threatening way, as they navigate questions and explore their personal responsibility regarding respect for others. Dr. Podgurski and the beloved Nonnie, guide us with insight and sensitivity to recognize our own *privilege* and demonstrate how we might all become stronger allies for one another.

As with every volume in the series, Dr. Podgurski and the wise Nonnie provide us with the guidance we need to be wiser and kinder members of society.

Parents, grandparents, educators and all nurturers need to add this volume to their collection.

~ **Nancy Aloi, M. Ed.,** Educator

The Nonnie Series does it again. An amazing resource, *Nonnie Talks about Disability* supports navigating challenging but necessary conversations about centering disabled young people. This book is an excellent tool for putting into practice, "every person is a person of worth". I encourage folks to read and utilize the disability justice framework in their professional and personal lives. Thank you, Kendle and Nonnie!

~ **Cindy Lee Alves, M.Ed.,** Sexuality Educator

Dr. Podgurski and Kendle crafted a wonderful piece that introduces young people to understanding how someone experiences disability and accessibility, as well as ableism, through story based on real people. As all *Nonnie* books do, the focus is on the young person's experience and interpretation of the world and helping the move from understanding their own experience, to building the skills to see and appreciate the experience of others. A resource for all learners alike.

Jeffrey W. Anthony, CHES

  AcademyPress ~ http://www.healthyteens.com/

Endorsements

I just finished reading *Nonnie Talks about Disability.* WONDERFUL!!!! Before reading it, I envisioned my own children as they were growing up and questions they had when they saw someone with a disability and the curious questions they would ask. Truly, the book touched on all the things I was looking for- the pointing, the questioning, the confusion and the curiosity. It addressed all of those things. I also loved the spectrum of disabilities covered.

~ **Heather Crowe**, MA Counseling

I happily offer this endorsement for yet another volume in the series of "Nonnie Talks About" books, the work of the astonishing Dr. Mary Jo Podgurski. This time, Nonnie – a.k.a. Dr. P. - introduces some new characters and a new issue for young people to tackle: how to understand, how to respond to, and how to respectfully support individuals living with differences that may be less obvious than gender or skin color — like Down syndrome — as well as ones that are very obvious — like using a wheelchair — in ways that are perhaps kinder and more honest than popular culture seems to model.

This book is one we didn't even know we needed, perhaps because we didn't want to know, staying stuck in our own discomfort. Yet children, from very young ages, do notice these differences, and adults so often struggle with how to answer their questions, because we don't know the answers!

But once again, Nonnie, rather than rushing in with her own answers, shows us how to guide young people to create their own answers. There is no better way to educate. Thank you again, Nonnie! What will you teach us next?

~ **Joan Garrity,** Educator and Trainer

We are so lucky to add another amazing resource to our roles of working with students! Mary Jo brings a reality to each book she develops and allows children and adults to have the difficult conversations that are so necessary to accept one another.

~ **Christy Lewis,** LCCW

Thank you for writing this book and showing Society we are real people with real emotions, wants and desires like them. People with disabilities are just like them, we just have a different set of circumstances to overcome

~ **Mike Matthews,** Pastor

A great book that teaches the youth about acceptance, inclusion and respect. Dr. Mary Jo Podgurski truly believes each person is a person of worth. Her passion to encourage and empower people of all abilities is evident throughout her Nonnie series.

~ **Darrilyn McCrerey, B.A.,** Art Therapy

77

Endorsements

I have been instructing Healthy Relationships, Substance Abuse Prevention (Alcohol and Other Drugs), and Human Sexuality for over 10 years at the college level, and recently began instructing in elementary and middle school health programs. I have loved sharing the Nonnie series with students in our health education and teacher preparation courses. I have seen them learn so much about not only the topic areas, but also ways to respect young people and nurture connections and critical thinking simultaneously. I have wished for this book for use in my own home and also to share with students on the teaching career path. I am so glad it is finally here! I am excited to share this book with my colleagues in adaptive physical education and teacher preparation. This book is a terrific tool for parents and teachers to help navigate these topics in a respectful and thoughtful conversation with kids. My third grade son enjoys Nonnie books at bedtime when we are able to actually talk about these topics. I appreciate the back up in answering the tough questions. Dr. Podgurski's book has positively contributed to my own confidence, competence, and capabilities as an educator and a parent.

~Shawn Sellers M.Ed., CHES
Instructor of Community Health, Western Oregon University

Author's Note about the next reviewer: *I spoke at a national conference a year ago and was at dinner. I heard whispers behind me, and suddenly a lovely young person was standing beside me! She wanted to share that she was a big fan of my Nonnie books! We had a delightful conversation and I asked her if she'd like to review the next book in the series. She said yes, and here are her words! It's really cool to have such a great fan!*

Thank you, Sarah!

One of the things I really like about this disabilities book is that it really explains how to interact with people with disabilities. How to be polite and that they are a person just like you and me. I like the way Nonnie's books give us time to reflect about what we just learned. I like the way that Dr. Podgurski puts the same people in the story each time, I like learning different things with them and I like the way she talks with them. Nonnie helps me feel more comfortable with these awkward topics. Thank you Dr. Podgurski!

~ **Sarah N. Slough,** Sixth Grader

The *Nonnie Talks About* series continues to be a groundbreaker of inclusive storytelling for children grades 3-8, ensuring that all young people are represented and visible. The latest volume, *Nonnie Talks About DisAbility,* centers students with characteristics traditionally known as disabilities and emphasizes the *abilities* they have. Students learn that each and every person is worthy a recurring theme throughout the series, and to treat everyone with respect.

~ **Bill Taverner, M.Ed.**

   AcademyPress ~ http://www.healthyteens.com/

Dr. Mary Jo Podgurski is the founder and director of The Washington Health System Teen Outreach and the Academy for Adolescent Health in Washington, Pa.

She is a nurse, a counselor, a parent, a trainer and speaker, and an educator who is dedicated to serving young people. The Outreach has reached over 250,000 young people since 1988. Check out www.healthyteens.com for information on the Academy and its programs.

Dr. Podgurski is certified as a childbirth educator through Lamaze International, as a sexuality educator and a sexuality counselor through AASECT (American Association for Sexuality Educators, Counselors and Therapists) as an Olweus Bullying Prevention Program trainer and through Parents As Teachers.

She is an authorized facilitator for the Darkness to Light abuse prevention program and a certified trainer for the Olweus Bullying Prevention Program. Dr. Mary Jo is the author of the *Ask Mary Jo* weekly column in the *Observer-Reporter* newspaper and answers 6—10 questions from young people daily. She wrote *Nonnie Talks about Gender* in 2014 as a labor of love and TheNonnie Series™ was birthed!

Most importantly, Dr. Mary Jo and her partner Rich are the parents of three wonderful adult children and are blessed to be grandparents. She is a Nonnie in Real Life!

Dr. Podgurski believes ally is a verb.
She believes in social and racial justice.
She believes in young people.
She believes each person is a person of worth. Please pass it on.

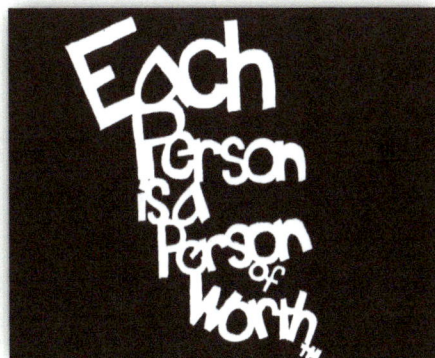

 AcademyPress ~ http://www.healthyteens.com/

ABOUT THE NONNIE SERIES

The **Nonnie**Series

Writing *Nonnie Talks about Gender* in the summer of 2014 was a true labor of love. The idea of a "Nonnie Series" never entered my mind. The reactions to *Nonnie Talks about Gender* surprised and humbled me. I began to realize gender wasn't the only challenging topic in our world. Social media and 24-hour news have created information overload, where even elementary school children are inundated with potentially confusing and troubling subjects. How should adults open the door to these teachable moments?

As a young nurse I became a birth advocate; as a certified Lamaze childbirth educator I have continued my commitment to birthing women and families since the 1970s. In 1973, I began working with pediatric oncology at Memorial Sloan Kettering Cancer Center in New York City. My passion for birthing normally dovetailed with my growing commitment for death with dignity. I became a hospice nurse in the 1980s. Long before the "circle of life" became part of a popular film for children, I learned how vital birth and death are to the human experience...and how often both topics are avoided when talking with children. With birth and death advocacy as my foundation, I decided to tackle these subjects in books for children as part of a series based on the "Nonnie" concept. Then, life intervened.

As an ally and advocate for racial and social justice, I cannot ignore how much our culture needs to address racial equity. Then, as I was presenting my child abuse prevention program, *Inside Out, Your Body is Amazing Inside and Out and Belongs Only to YOU*, an eight-year-old child told me what #BlackLivesMatter meant to her. We talked, I listened. This little one's very real fear that her own life was less worthy than another's based on the color of her skin was my inspiration for *Nonnie Talks about Race*.

Nonnie Talks about Puberty was born because another child needed it. I began teaching growing up classes called "What's Up as You Grow Up" in 1984. Gender non-conforming children are often confused during puberty; I couldn't find an inclusive resource on growing up, so I wrote one. Empathy is a learned skill. I hope all children will benefit from the book.

I then completed *Nonnie Talks about Pregnancy and Birth* and *Nonnie Talks about Death*. As a sexologist, *Nonnie Talks about Sex...& More*, was a no-brainer for my next book. *Nonnie Talks about Trauma* was written as a direct result to young people's reactions to the Parkland shooting. I tried to offer a balanced approach. The Let's Talk program really happened in our community. *Nonnie Talks about Consent* and *Nonnie Talks about Disability* came from the needs of children and young people today. I have a list of other topics I hope to explore.

If you have any ideas for the "Nonnie Series," or would like to be informed about coming titles, please connect with me at podmj@healthyteens.com.

79

AcademyPress ~ http://www.healthyteens.com/

Nonnie
Talks about
Gender

Suggested for children
in grades 3—8
and their trusted adults

An Interactive
Book for Children
and Adults

Written by Dr. Mary Jo Podgurski
Illustrations by Alice M. Burroughs
©2014 All rights reserved

Nonnie
Talks about
Puberty*

EACH PERSON IS A PERSON OF WORTH

Suggested for children
in grades 3—8
and their trusted adults

*For youth of all genders, including those who are transgender, gender fluid or questioning their gender.

An Interactive
Book for Children
and Adults

Written by Dr. Mary Jo Podgurski
Illustrations by Alice M. Burroughs

Nonnie
Talks about
Death

Suggested for children in grades
3-8 and their trusted adults

An Interactive
Book
for Children
and Adults

By Dr. Mary Jo Podgurski
Consultant Dr. Lisa Podgurski
Illustrations by Alice M. Burroughs

Nonnie
Talks about
Consent

Suggested for children in grades
3-8 and their trusted adults

An Interactive
Book
for Children
and Adults

By Dr. Mary Jo Podgurski
Consultant Dr. Lexx Brown-James
Illustrations by Alice M. Burroughs

Did you enjoy Nonnie Talks about disability?

Want to prepare children for relationships by
teaching with *Nonnie Talks about Consent*?
See the need for *Nonnie Talks about Trauma*?
Want to use *Nonnie Talks about Sex…& More*
to add to 'the talk' with a young person?
Can you use *Nonnie Talks about Death* in your family?
Interested in *Nonnie Talks about Puberty*?
Curious about *Nonnie Talks about Race*?
Intrigued by *Nonnie Talks about Pregnancy and Birth*?
Wonder about *Nonnie Talks about Gender*?
Entranced by the concept of the Nonnie Series?

Dr. Podgurski has dedicated her
life to empowering young people.
She strives to model her motto of
"Each Person is a Person of Worth"
through education, writing, and trainings.
She is available for workshops and consultation.
She is also the author of 34 books.
You can find her books, including the Nonnie Series,
at Amazon or on her website,
drmaryjopodgurski.com
You can reach her at:
Email: podmj@healthyteens.con
http://www.healthyteens.com/
Toll free #: 1 (888) 301-2311
Twitter DrMaryJoPod

Future titles in The Nonnie Series™
Nonnie Talks about Relationships
Nonnie Talks about Cancer
Nonnie Talks about Mental Health

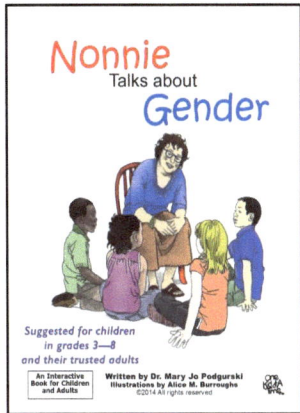

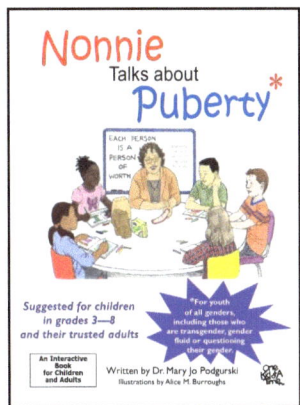

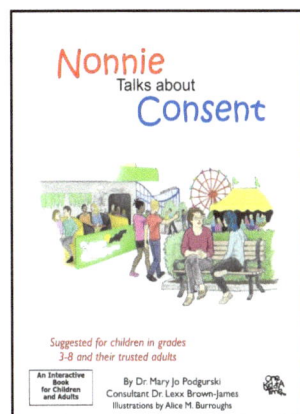

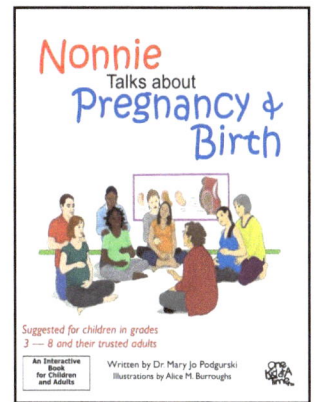

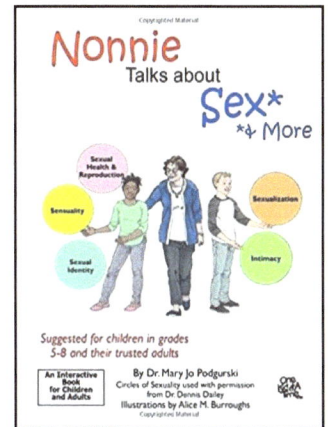

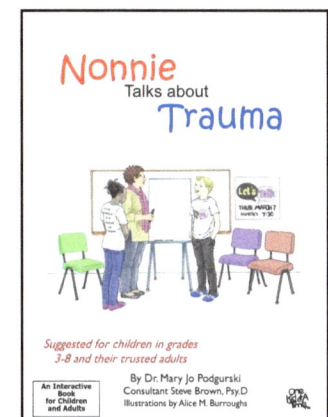

Nonnie
Talks about
Pregnancy & Birth

Suggested for children in grades
3 — 8 and their trusted adults

An Interactive
Book
for Children
and Adults

Written by Dr. Mary Jo Podgurski
Illustrations by Alice M. Burroughs

Nonnie
Talks about
Race

Suggested for children in grades
3-8 and their trusted adults

An Interactive
Book
for Children
and Adults

Written Dr. Mary Jo Podgurski
with Tanya M. Bass, MS, CHES and
Mariotta Gary-Smith, MPH
Illustrations by Alice M. Burroughs

Copyrighted Material

Nonnie
Talks about
Sex*
*& More

Sexual Health & Reproduction

Sensuality

Sexualization

Sexual Identity

Intimacy

Suggested for children in grades
5-8 and their trusted adults

An Interactive
Book
for Children
and Adults

By Dr. Mary Jo Podgurski
Circles of Sexuality used with permission
from Dr. Dennis Dailey
Illustrations by Alice M. Burroughs

Copyrighted Material

Nonnie
Talks about
Trauma

Suggested for children in grades
3-8 and their trusted adults

An Interactive
Book
for Children
and Adults

By Dr. Mary Jo Podgurski
Consultant Steve Brown, Psy.D
Illustrations by Alice M. Burroughs

79

AcademyPress ~ http://www.healthyteens.com/

www.ingramcontent.com/pod-product-compliance
Lightning Source LLC
Chambersburg PA
CBHW060811270326
41928CB00003B/56